BETRAYED

ADDITIONAL PRAISE
FOR BETRAYED

This book—from the heartfelt stories of betrayal to the useful checklists—would have been helpful to have when my family was financially betrayed as direct investors in several Bernie Madoff funds.
TODDI GUTNER, global innovation lead for Firmenich

You just can't put this book down—there has never been one like it. Like air, betrayal surrounds us, yet we often don't recognize it for what it is until it's too late—the ultimate destruction of trust. The stories are shocking. In my career as a crisis manager, I sometimes think I've seen it all, but nothing cuts, destroys, and lingers like betrayal. Susan and Elaine get it, explain it, and show us how to not only survive betrayal, but how to keep our love, joy, and trust alive even while doing so. A must read in our crazy, inconstant world.
DAVIA TEMIN, CEO of Temin and Company, a crisis, reputation, and corporate culture consultancy, also serving as a leadership coach to C-Suite executives and boards

Often betrayal, large and small, haunts us through our daily lives. By sharing real-life stories in an intimate and personal tone, Elaine and Susan provide us with essential tools to help us work through them. You won't stop reading, and you will realize that the strength of others empowers all of us.
ANA PAULA PESSOA, chair of Kunumi AI, director of Crédit Suisse, News Corporation and Vinci Group

Susan Stautberg and Elaine Eisenman have collaborated on an important topic no one wants to talk about but everyone has experienced multiple times in their lives: being betrayed. This thoughtful book of case studies and sound advice on how to deal with different types of hurtful behavior by those we trust and care about provides the right balance of introspection and external insights. A must read to help us know we aren't alone in working through these tough events and that we can also get to the other side with the ability to mitigate the risk of betrayal in the future and to have more resilience if we get caught up in it again.

MAGGIE WILDEROTTER, chairman and CEO of Grand Reserve Inn; corporate boards including Lyft, Costco Wholesale Corporation, Hewlett Packard Enterprise, Cadence Design Systems, and DocuSign

BETRAYED

A SURVIVOR'S GUIDE TO
LYING, CHEATING, & DOUBLE DEALING

Elaine Eisenman, PhD & Susan Stautberg
with Lynn G. Poekel

Published by Advantage, Charleston, South Carolina.
Member of Advantage Media Group.

ADVANTAGE is a registered trademark, and the Advantage colophon is a trademark of Advantage Media Group, Inc.

Printed in the United States of America.

10 9 8 7 6 5 4 3 2 1

ISBN: 978-1-64225-104-3
LCCN: 2019940194

Book design by Carly Blake.
Cover illustration by Chuck Wojtkiewicz.

Dedication

SUSAN

The idea for this book came from a surprise girls' birthday weekend that Julia Hansen held for me. As we talked about our lives and realized that we had all been betrayed, we decided to collect and share stories and advice to help others avoid being hurt—or to at least survive and thrive afterward. As Vernon Law counsels, "Experience is a hard teacher because she gives the test first, the lesson afterward."

Antonyms for betrayal (honesty, loyalty, truthfulness, openness) best describe the attributes of my partners, Elaine Eisenman and Lynn G. Poekel; those who shared their stories for this book; and mostly, my family—Edward, Rachel, and my mother—and close friends. To all, I give my endless gratitude.

You helped us realize there are no failures in life, just detours you didn't expect.

ELAINE

My deepest gratitude to all those who contributed to this book. I am humbled by your extraordinary generosity of spirit and desire to help others learn from your tough lessons of experience.

And to my family, for their ideas and support. To Steven for your love, laughter, ideas, support, and willingness and ability to always consider, reality check, and make possible my "what ifs."

To my amazing children, Jessica, Peter, Matthew, and David, for the wonderful distractions of family texts, for your willingness to tolerate my advice, and for the joy we share in each other.

To Simon, my loving and extraordinary grandson, for keeping us all laughing and learning about the world from your very unique perspective.

LYNN

To my husband Charlie for all your love, humor, and support. May you never betray me!

Table of Contents

ACKNOWLEDGMENTS XI

INTRODUCTION 1
Why We Wrote This Book

CHAPTER ONE 11
Why Betrayal Cuts So Deep

CHAPTER TWO 27
Red Flags? What Red Flags?
I Never Saw 'Em Coming

CHAPTER THREE 53
Betrayed? Never Surrender Your Power
or Your Soul

CHAPTER FOUR 73
The Family Business: A Hotbed of Betrayal

CHAPTER FIVE 93
Yes, Revenge Is Sweet, but Karma Is Sweeter

CHAPTER SIX 115
To Forgive or Not to Forgive, That Is the Question

CHAPTER SEVEN 135
**Resilience—What Doesn't Kill You
Makes You Stronger**

CHAPTER EIGHT .161
Betrayal—Lessons from the War Zone

EPILOGUE 185

ABOUT THE AUTHORS 193

CONTACT US 199

BOOK CLUB QUESTIONS 201

BIBLIOGRAPHY 203

Acknowledgments

We would like to thank all the exceptional people without whom this book could never have been written.

First and foremost are our survivors of betrayal. Their willingness to share their stories in order to help others benefit from their very tough and painful lessons demonstrates an extraordinary generosity of spirit that we will never forget. Because we have promised anonymity to our survivor-storytellers, we will list them here by the names they were given in their stories. In order of occurrence in our book, our deepest gratitude to: Sophia, Jenny, Ingrid, Dr. Samuels, Gina, Priscilla, Leslie, Andy, Jeremy, Ellie, Debra, Liz, Kerry, Carlos, Mimi, Carolyn, Tara, Austin, Amy, Casey, Allen, Patty, Carly, Tracey, Richard, Miranda, Nancy, Andrew, Bridget, Karen, Jessica, Hallie, Mimi, Matthew, Debra, and Robert.

Each of you know which story is your own. Our deepest gratitude for sharing your story and your insights.

We also want to thank Dr. Susan Erstling, Jenny Sanford, Dr. Jose Stevens, and Marcy Syms for their wisdom and perspectives on the nature of betrayal and the best ways to move forward.

Thank you also to Chuck Wojtkiewicz for creating our attention-grabbing cover image; thank you to Leslie Dube, Ellen Dube, and Jordan Williams for their administrative support; and thank you to the entire Advantage team including Nick Read, Kristin Goodale, and Kelly Perry. Thank you also to Cathy Allen, Dr. Lilie van Arsdall, and Naomi McDougall Jones for sharing their marketing advice and ideas.

We are very grateful for the generous support from our testimonial writers, Lauren C. Anderson, Colleen Ammerman, Dr. Helen Fisher, Dr. Boris Groysberg, Toddi Gutner, Ana Paula Pessoa, Valerie Plame, Davia Temin, and Maggie Wilderotter.

Last but not least, our thanks to our readers who were instrumental in keeping us focused on our mission: Elizabeth Brooks, Diane Danielson, Matthew Eisenman, Steven Eisenman, Rosemary Harder, Shaunna Jones, Kate Keough, Jill Kanin Lovers, Lara Metcalf, Jean Matthews, Erin McCormick, Edward Stautberg, and last, but by no means least, Dr. Rachel Stautberg.

INTRODUCTION

Why We Wrote This Book

There are some things you learn best in the calm, and some in the storm.
—Willa Cather, *The Song of the Lark*

I magine the following scenarios: A longtime friend and colleague steals your job while you are on medical leave. Your spouse humiliates you while carrying on an extended affair. A trusted advisor tries to force your board to fire you. A longtime office manager robs your medical practice of hundreds of thousands of dollars.

Could any of these events happen to you? Have they? Will they? Sadly, the answer is often yes—because betrayal is part of life.

Who hasn't felt the sting of betrayal: the shame of being thrown to the wolves by a lifelong friend, sibling, lover, or colleague? There is a reason "Et tu, Brute?" is the most celebrated expression of betrayal: it's because betrayal is an ugly universal truth to which no one is immune.

Contained in this book are real-life stories of betrayal in love, business, marriage, family, and friendship. When we began our quest for stories, we were amazed by the outpouring of people's darkest secrets, as well as the all too common "Talk to so-and-so because he has a great one" and "Here's a story you won't believe."

Everyone was convinced that his or her tale of betrayal was the worst. Ego? Or testament to the pain and hurt?

As we heard stories from friends, strangers, and colleagues, we came to discover that there is no practical guide for surviving betrayal and then moving beyond it with one's strength and dignity intact. Navigating the trauma is just the beginning. Determining how to build resilience, courage, and strength is even more important. And that is our goal: to give you a road map. To make you a survivor who thrives in a new and better future.

In the past, the shame of betrayal most often elicited silence, but now, with the #MeToo culture in full swing, those days are over. Bad behavior is under a klieg light and betrayers are called out on their deeds. We received that message loud and clear from over sixty people who answered our request for interviews. We also turned to psychological, sociological, and legal research on betrayal in order to better understand and expand the concepts our interviews revealed.

And to share our insights and to help you move forward, we wrote this book.

The following are a few organizing principles about our book. In the coming chapters, you will read the full stories of those previously mentioned and more, as well as learn ways to avoid betrayal and cope with it when it can't be escaped. While each story is true, we have changed the names, locations, and all identifying information of the individuals, as we promised each contributor complete anonymity.

First, we want you to understand the nature of betrayal and why it cuts us to the core. Our focus is on intentional betrayal, where there is no doubt that the betrayer set out to cause some form of harm to the person betrayed. It is all about trust and what happens when someone trusts blindly—and why you must learn to use only *wise* trust in all your relationships.

Next comes the importance of trusting your gut. It can sensitize you to red flags and help you avoid betrayal, or the very least, minimize its impact.

Family betrayal gets its own chapter because those knotty relationships make for a high degree of intrigue.

The usual suspects of betrayal in love, marriage, business, and friendship are also topics we cover throughout.

We'll then move on to dealing with the aftermath of betrayal by using essential tools—like forgiveness—and reclaiming your power to move on. We'll also look at forgiveness's evil twin, which is revenge, and discuss why it may or may not be your best option. We'll learn how victimhood can transform into confidence, giving you the courage to move forward.

So what makes us experts on betrayal? For one, all three of us have our own stories (see the following). But we do bring other credentials to the table.

Elaine Eisenman, PhD, is an organizational psychologist, board member, former executive and dean, wife, mother, and grandmother who has spent her career advising corporate and academic transitions. She has witnessed betrayal of trust at every level and has both seen and experienced the turmoil it creates.

ELAINE'S STORY:
THE JEWELRY STORE

"Don't worry," said John to my parents. "I'll make sure she stays safe when she works for me this summer in Boston. No creep will come near her!"
I was young, three months short of turning sixteen, and eager to work in the city for the summer. No more camp counselor jobs! My parents were reluctant to let me take the train into the city and be on my own. I managed to convince them to do just that, however, when I asked an old, dear family friend if I could work in his jewelry store in downtown Boston, close to the train station. I was so excited when he said yes and they agreed to let me go. It was my first stab at independence, and I was thrilled by the prospect of freedom.

The betrayal of my young trust came fast and quick on the day I started work.

Thrilled by my first sale, I rushed to the back of the store to have a pair of earrings gift wrapped for my customer.

John, the owner, shared my excitement and gave me a big, burly hug.

In a flash, his hands reached up my dress and down into my underpants.

He was a groper, eager to fondle the new employee. I was in total shock, sickened by this physical betrayal.

His wife ignored what was going on as she finished gift wrapping the package. She even stepped back for a moment to admire her handiwork.

In a cloud of disgust, I ran to the front of the store, put the gift-wrapped package into a nice bag, and handed it to the waiting customer.

The senior salesgirl, who was all of twenty, knew exactly what had happened. My face said it all, and her experience working for the owner had left no doubt in her mind.

"Welcome to the club, Elaine," she said sympathetically. "This is just a summer job for you. You don't have to take it, so just quit and walk

away," she advised. "You don't need this job like I do."

But I couldn't walk out after just one day because I didn't know what I would tell my parents. As humiliating and devastating as this betrayal had been, I just couldn't tell them. After all, the owner and his wife were their longtime friends. Would my parents even believe me?

So I made the decision to protect my parents from John's disgusting behavior and I learned how to protect myself from his quick and grabby hands.

I made it through the summer, ultimately avoiding any more back-room groping. Outrunning the owner's hands was just as important as the two critical lessons I learned: Trust must be earned, never freely given. And even people who seem wonderful may have a very dark side.

* * *

Susan Stautberg is a senior executive and strategist whose global career has spanned corporate, entrepreneurial, political, and government entities, including the White House. She's a mom, a widow, and a founder of two international organizations. Throughout her life, she's witnessed and experienced betrayal up close and personal.

SUSAN'S STORY:
HE JUST WASN'T WORTH IT

I was in my twenties, working in Washington, DC, as a White House Fellow. It was an exciting time because I was helping to write policy and communicating the administration's initiatives in different public venues.

One afternoon, having delivered a public-policy speech, I spotted Will, a man I was currently dating, in the audience. My initial reaction was, how great that he came to hear my talk! After the speech, I quickly moved through the crowd. It was then I noticed the attractive woman at his side.

I pushed through the crowd before Will and his companion could make a hasty exit.

"Hello, Will. So glad you and your friend could make it," I said with all the enthusiasm I could muster.

Before he could respond, I introduced myself to Jane. She had an open manner and seemed eager to talk.

"Susan, ever since Will and I started seeing each other, he has told me all about your first-rate public-speaking abilities." She looked down at her shoes and continued, "It's something Will thinks I can improve on."

"What a compliment," I said, "but I assure you Jane, there are simple techniques that are a snap to learn."

I quietly passed Jane my card and she gave me hers. The three of us then said good-bye and went on our way.

While I ignored Will's calls (which I knew would be full of insincere explanations), I immediately got in touch with Jane.

I learned she already held down an important job at the White House. She had an impressive resume and a list of accomplishments achieved at a relatively young age, while I offered career advice as well as those famous public-speaking tips.

As our friendship developed, I let Jane know Will had been dating me at the same time he'd been seeing her. She took the news well.

"I appreciate your honesty, Susan. His behavior has left a lot to be desired."

We bonded over Will's cheating ways, dropped him from our lives, and never heard another word from the double-dealer.

"Jane, I promise to introduce you to a far more reputable guy," I told her.

"Susan, I accept the challenge," she laughed.

I later introduced Jane to a man in New York City, and they've been married for over thirty years.

Personal experience taught me that a betrayal can have positive results, as long as you read the red flags.

To this day, I remain good friends with Jane and her husband.

* * *

Lynn Poekel is a creative director who has seen betrayal as a daily operating principle in the advertising industry. In between treacheries, she introduced women to "Maybe She's Born With It. Maybe It's Maybelline." and wrote ad copy for Diet Coke, Johnson & Johnson, Heineken, Macy's, and more.

LYNN'S STORY:
IT'S NOT PERSONAL; IT'S BUSINESS

Six months after he arrived at the agency, the new CEO invited me to a meeting. I entered the office and was surprised to see the head of HR and my account partner, Sandy, waiting for me.

This, I knew, was the beginning of the end.

As I listened to a litany of my shortcomings, my friend, my counterpart, my confidant for over thirty years, Sandy greeted me with a half-hearted wave.

Sandy and I had risen in the ranks together—she, working hard as a strategist, and I, as a creative director. We knew each other's secrets and strengths. We even led a $600 million agency together.

Through the years, I watched her chastise fearful subordinates, rationalize bad behavior, and refuse to take blame for any failure.

She had a marvelous ability to deflect. I ignored it all because I appreciated her smarts and thought, I'll never get that treatment.

It was clear the new CEO wanted me out, but I'd never thought Sandy would betray me by creating a phony crisis that would lead to my demise.

It all happened over a digital banner. My apparent dereliction of duty involved a lack of "quality" attention to a single assignment.

Before talking to me, Sandy ran to the CEO. (What a great opportunity to sabotage the creative director and serve the CEO's agenda!) Both of them demanded a reorganization of the creative department: new staff, new proposals.

Of course, I did the work. Late one night, I walked into Sandy's office to ask her what was going on: the truth, the real deal.

Silence. A smile. Some meaningless chitchat. And then this came out of her mouth:

"Don't you think it'd be great to have a couple of months off and be paid for it?"

I knew what was next.

The day of my firing, Sandy was conveniently out of town. Afterward she called repeatedly and sent a flurry of emails. I turned off my voicemail and deleted my messages.

I never responded to Sandy's overtures because I had heard all her toxic explanations before, especially, "It's not personal; it's business." But the truth is, it was personal.

Happily, I've continued to work in the industry and have been surrounded by great minds and far less duplicity. Sandy may have betrayed me, but she never robbed me of my love for the business.

* * *

In this book, we hope to give you a positive road map to the future. It's summarized in the acronym "BOUNCE." Our book will help you become:

- Bold in asserting what is important and necessary for your survival.

- Optimistic about the future and unwilling to let others cloud your vision with their concern.

- Undaunted in finding your safe space.

- Nimble in recognizing opportunities for your future.

- Courageous in defending your value and holding on to your identity.

- Empowered to become the person you want to be.

We have found there is no single best way to design a new future post-betrayal, but there are keys within each successful story—keys that you can apply to your unique situation to help you unlock a brighter future.

Now let's begin.

CHAPTER ONE

Why Betrayal Cuts So Deep

Let's dive right in with Sophia's story.

BETRAYAL WRIT LARGE

It was an awful death for her husband of thirty-five years. Pain, drugs, and the amputation of both legs. Sitting in her lawyer's office with her husband's trustee, Sophia thought it would finally be over after the reading of the will.

Of course, Sophia knew the contents. That had been the subject of many of her conversations with her dying husband. He'd even offered to buy her a larger house. But as the dutiful wife who hadn't wanted to cause her husband added strife, she'd graciously refused.

Henry, the lawyer, was fidgety. He coughed once or twice, then said to the trustee, "Are you going to handle this? Good. I'll leave."

Henry couldn't get out of the room fast enough. That's when Sophia locked eyes with the trustee and heard him say …

"It seems there was another woman in your husband's life, and he left her over $3 million dollars."

The news of this betrayal left Sophia pinned to her chair. As she gathered what was left of her dignity, she found her voice and thanked the trustee.

The drive home from Santa Barbara to Montecito was a short one. But it gave her time to ponder so many questions.

What would she tell the children? Who was the woman? A mistress? How did this happen? When did it happen?

Sophia had convinced herself that she and her husband were happy, and in love. They'd had a passion for riding in the mountains. They'd even raised horses and showed them. In fact, they had often considered the idea of buying a small ranch in San Ysidro, but the siren call of the arts and social life in Montecito had kept them there.

Sophia's stepchildren were outraged by the revelation in their father's will. They wanted to sue because it was their grandmother's money their father was handing out to a mistress, and by all rights, it needed to be kept in the family.

The suit never came to be because the woman in question decided to return the money to the trust. Through her lawyer, she communicated that her reputation meant more to her than the money.

Deep in mourning and depressed, Sophia sought the help of a therapist. Through this three-year process, she'd come to realize there were parts of her relationship that she'd willfully chosen to "block out."

Like that night at the opera when a friend asked Sophia, "Who was that attractive young woman I saw your husband with at the San Diego horse show?"

Or the anonymous letter saying her husband was having an affair and had promised to marry the woman.

Or the check for $50,000 written out to cash.

Or the rumors of a relationship with an intern their daughter's age.

Or the myriad country club dinners Sophia was not a part of.

With each nasty discovery, Sophia had confronted her husband.

Denial followed, as did a battery of excuses.

"It was lunch with a business associate. For heaven's sake, there's no affair."

In horror, she learned that before her husband's terminal diagnosis, he had purchased a house for his mistress a mere five blocks from his home with Sophia, which provided a convenient way for him to add sex to his daily jogging routine.

Sophia then realized that while her husband was dying in the hospital, the $3 million mistress had disguised herself as his nutritionist and stayed with her husband after Sophia had left for the day. The staff had told her that the door to her husband's room was always closed when the "nutritionist" paid her nightly visits.

Sophia had wrapped herself in a cloud of denial when each fact presented itself. She'd also refused to see a pattern of infidelity in her husband's behavior that was obvious even at the start of their courtship. She'd packed it away because her desire for them to be a couple had been greater than her sense of self-worth.

Today, after much therapeutic work and deep soul searching, Sophia has found the power to believe in herself. She is much quicker to pick up on signals and confront bad behavior. She has learned from her crushing betrayal and moved on to living a life with confidence.

Her one regret? Not having taken her husband up on that big new house!

Sophia's betrayal is one hell of a trifecta of lies, treachery, and deceit. It embraces everything from deathbed infidelity to financial duplicity.

We all have words for betrayal, but a true definition is more nuanced. There is a sliding scale of the act, from lies of omission to deeds worthy of Iago, Shakespeare's most sinister villain, who betrayed Othello's trust. And while Sophia's story isn't equal to anything the bard described, we have learned that any and all violations of trust on the continuum of betrayal cut deeply. The emotional impact of any form of betrayal is devastating.

Why?

Because betrayal destroys trust. And since trust is the foundation of all relationships, you can see why betrayal does such damage. Without trust, relationships are impossible—so without trust, betrayal is impossible.

We're smart enough to know people will always look out for their own best interests, but in turn, in any relationship, we believe others will respect and honor *our* interests. Unfortunately, that's not always the case.

Betrayal lurks in the shadows of trust, just waiting to spring on our good faith. And the deeper the bond of trust, the greater the pain of betrayal, because a strong bond carries with it inherent vulnerability. The Latin derivation here is highly relevant: *vulnerare* means "to wound, hurt, injure, or maim."[1] Vulnerability sits conveniently between betrayal and trust as yet another element in the mix. In order to trust, we must allow ourselves to be vulnerable.

But there's more.

Trust breaks down into different categories. Based on the work of Dr. Steven Stosny, a psychologist and author who treats people for anger and relationship problems, we will begin with *blind trust*. As he notes, "Blind trust puts faith in someone without regard to demonstrated reliability or trustworthiness. It's more a reluctance

---

1   Kaufman and Schipper, *Teaching with Compassion: An Educator's Oath to Teach from the Heart*.

to experience the doubt, anxiety, and loneliness of distrust than an endorsement of the other person's better qualities."[2]

Sophia perfectly illustrated this by refusing to see a pattern in her husband's behavior. She chose to remain married despite the doubts she held about his fidelity.

Blind trust is not only a danger in love, but also in friendship.

Ben's story is a good example of blind trust given in friendship.

THE BEST FRIEND A GUY COULD HAVE ... OR WAS HE?

"Hank, how could you be so deliberately underhanded?" Ben demanded. "How could you bring in another partner for the buyout and not say a word to me?"

Hank responded smoothly, "When we talked about the future of the company, I couldn't get a fix on whether or not you wanted to be part of the new entity."

"That is just plain wrong, Hank. One easy way to get an answer would have been to simply ask me."

Ben grabbed his laptop, left the room, and exited the building. He needed to think and piece together the events that led to this betrayal.

Walking into Starbucks, Ben ordered a strong coffee, sat down, and tried to recall whether or not he had seen Hank behave so deceitfully in all the years he'd known him.

They'd had a long history together. The two of them had been great friends at a Big Ten university. Both had been serious students, involved in lots of campus activities and a few clever start-ups to earn spending money. They'd believed in focused energy and having fun. Hank had always had a genial way of always getting what he wanted without

---

2   Stosny, "Trust Wisely: Living and Loving after Betrayal."

ruffling any feathers.

Thirty years after graduation, they were still friends. Hank had turned his attention to becoming the CEO of a fast-growing start-up. He'd wisely realized that growth required him to focus externally, and so had a proposition for his investment partners.

"We need a president who will take over the day-to-day functions. Then I can focus on outside opportunities, and the new person can make them operational," he recommended.

His partners agreed.

Hank knew that his longtime friend Ben had just taken another company through to sale and had his eye out for a new opportunity. He believed that with Ben at the helm, the company would be in steady hands and would thrive.

"This is a real chance for you to be a driving force in my business. I can step back and you can run it. Operations is your forte, not mine. Hey, this'll be fun. Remember fun?" Hank winked.

Prohibited by his former company's contract to become a full-time employee of another company for three years, Ben happily signed on as a long-term consultant with a generous retainer. No equity was possible, as it was premature for him to become a partner.

As Ben and Hank talked about the future of the company, Ben's expectation was that he would ultimately become a partner with an equity stake in return for growing the business.

While Hank focused on building outside relationships, Ben ground out sixteen-hour days managing business operations to ensure steady growth.

Over the next year, the two of them had many conversations about how far the company could drive growth, and where the most potential lay. Hank decided he wanted to buy out the other partners and would put a plan in place to get it done.

"Just make sure I'm part of that plan," Ben said.

"Do you really have to ask?" Hank responded.

Months followed in which Ben and Hank worked side by side to see Hank's vision come to life. But Hank was uncharacteristically vague and wouldn't commit to Ben's role in the new entity. Ben felt a little warning bell ring, but attributed Hank's silence to work demands. After all, he and Hank had been close friends for over thirty years. He believed that their long and enduring friendship was his protection.

All along, Ben had assumed Hank was buying out the partners on his own. Every one of their conversations implied as much.

One day, Hank said to Ben, "My new partner is coming in at two o'clock today. I'd like you to meet him."

Hank had cut a deal with someone else to buy out the original partners—and he'd done so behind Ben's back and right under his nose.

Game, set, match.

Ben realized he had been used to build the business and prepare for the buyout. There would be no additional equity, and he was being tossed to the curb.

Ben resigned immediately. No rage. No equity payout. Just a fast exit. He'd learned a tough and expensive lesson. Not once did he regret the decision to leave and he went on to more positive and successful partnerships.

Ben's betrayal was a clear case of blind trust. Thirty years of friendship had clouded his thinking and caused him to ignore signs in Hank's behavior. Whether it was chasing travel upgrades or buying a car, Hank made sure he came out on top. Money wasn't the object, so much as inflating his sense of superiority. Despite Hank's arrogance, Ben had believed that loyalty and friendship were shared values, but had never tested his beliefs.

Going into business with friends or family should be a no-brainer, because these are the people to whom we are closest. Blind trust lulls us into thinking, "What's to worry about? It's friends! It's family!" In Chapter Four, we take a close look at the myth that family businesses are immune from betrayal.

Regardless of how well you may know someone, treat any business arrangement with due diligence. Do your homework and approach and proceed with caution because friendship or family ties are no guarantee against betrayal.

With the gift of hindsight, Ben realized that not only had he been naïve, but he'd also been a bit of an enabler. While he had stood by and watched Hank cut out other partners, he'd never suspected Hank would do the same to him. Ben had believed loyal friendship trumped all.

Ben learned the hard way that no one who blindly trusts another is immune from betrayal. Indeed, blind trust increases one's vulnerability.

Simply put, motives can be hidden, even with the best of friends. That's why it's smart to enter into any business relationship with eyes wide open, due diligence, caution, and friendship aside.

The second category of trust is *organizational trust*. This is based on the belief that we will all work together in the best interests of the organization, not just our own. And, in order to function at a high level, we need to believe that all our colleagues share that value.

We rely on the ethics and values of the company because we can't test the trustworthiness of all the individuals in an organization.

Ingrid's following story offers the perfect illustration of a violation of organizational trust.

A TRULY CRIMINAL BETRAYAL

Having always worked in the private sector, Ingrid had moved into the public sector to "make a difference." She accepted a position she recognized as a lateral move, but was convinced she could succeed in this new world. There was opportunity and a high level of visibility, and it all came quickly when Jim, her CEO, asked Ingrid to become CFO.

Her first challenge was to find an exceptional comptroller who would create and closely manage the municipal budget.

The CEO and Ingrid got the word out. Dozens of people had names to recommend and the resumes poured in. One proved to be just what they were looking for. Andy's strong financial and industry experience—as well as his amazing references—shot him to the top of the list.

"Andy came recommended by people you trust. He aced the interviews, Jim, and he's got a bright mind, so you should move quickly on this guy," Ingrid suggested.

She knew Jim was pleased, but she was also a stickler for vetting. The in-house HR team took over the review of Andy's background. Even though Ingrid typically performed reference checks herself, she quickly learned that, in the highly siloed public sector, HR alone typically handled this task. Interfering with their process was not welcome! Not wanting to appear overly aggressive, Ingrid stepped back. No red flags turned up. No question marks. So they were comfortable ending their due diligence and giving Andy the job.

Ingrid watched Andy's progress carefully. With his engaging personality and financial smarts, he soon became admired by his colleagues and relied on by his superiors.

So it was strange when Andy texted Ingrid, urgently asking her to meet him in the park. She couldn't imagine why he wanted such a private meeting, but she gave him the benefit of the doubt and grabbed her coat.

Andy was in shirtsleeves on that chilly November day and sweating bullets.

He coughed nervously and finally said, "I'm moving on, Ingrid. It's time."

"I hope it's something fantastic, Andy," she replied with a bit of surprise.

Andy refused to look at her. Instead, his eyes darted everywhere else. His discomfort was palpable.

"Well, we'll get to the details later," she said, hoping to relieve his anxiety.

Walking back to her office, she wondered what had turned her golden boy into a bundle of nerves. It didn't make any sense. But it didn't take long to discover the reason.

Days later, Andy was charged with white-collar crimes committed in another state. It was all over the news and social media. He'd clearly decided not to alert Ingrid or anyone else before he was arrested.

Dumbfounded, Ingrid called Jim.

"I heard it too," he said sadly. "This is a one heck of a public betrayal."

Ingrid flew into action, knowing the press would be demanding explanations. She helped hire outside investigators, who found Andy had padded his resume and was involved with a kickback scheme. Clearly, HR had not done as much diligence as Ingrid had believed.

But the fallout continued. Desperate people do desperate things, and Andy was no exception. He jumped bail and fled the state.

Ultimately, the United States government caught up with him, and he was sentenced to prison.

In the wake of Andy's betrayal, Ingrid felt angry and confused. At first, attention was focused on her. After all, she hired him. What should she have done differently? Lots of people had recommended Andy, not just her. Other people—including HR and outside legal investigators—were tasked with doing his background investigation. So why was everyone now trying to place the blame on her? She knew that she had done nothing wrong, other than, of course, trusting HR when they said his background check was clean.

Fortunately, Jim backed Ingrid entirely. He knew she was not at fault. Together, they launched a forensic audit and found that Andy had not abused his position within their organization. Although no financial problems surfaced, Ingrid still bears the scars of the whole experience.

But here, the case is not as cut and dry as Jim and the board had assumed. There were multiple betrayals. Ingrid had been cautious with Andy's hiring because she'd sensed his credentials were too good to be true. But despite her prior hands-on approach to checking references, she ignored her gut, followed the organization's rules, and ceded that responsibility to HR. When they found nothing, she relaxed and Andy was hired.

Ingrid choose the path of organizational trust, and waived any lingering disbelief about Andy's legitimacy. That's why this betrayal was so difficult for her. She was betrayed by HR, who did not perform the requisite comprehensive background check. She was betrayed by some of her colleagues, who wanted her to be the scapegoat. And she was betrayed by Andy, her superstar hire. Ingrid learned an important lesson. Even though you think you know a person, even though you trust and verify, if your gut tells you to dig deeper, do it. We'll return to this narrative later because it also illustrates a third form of trust we've yet to explain.

Next, Dr. Samuels's story mixes blind trust and organizational trust for a disastrous result.

PHYSICIAN, HEAL THYSELF

As Dr. Richard Samuels reached for his ringing cell phone, he glanced at his watch. It was two o'clock in the morning Tokyo time, and every cell of his jet-lagged body screamed.

On the other end of the line, was his accountant, Jason.

"Good God, Jason, what do you want? I AM ON HOLIDAY," he said with supreme irritation.

"Hey, Rick, I'm sorry, but you have to know what's going on," Jason replied.

The renowned Westchester plastic surgeon was in no mood for games.

"Give it to me fast so I can get back to sleep," Rick said.

"Your office manager, Yvonne, is nowhere to be found. I just got the call from your assistant, Julia."

Dr. Samuels fell back onto his pillow. Yvonne had been with him for ten years and handled the finances of his practice. She was his right hand, reliable backstop, and confidante. Without her, chaos reigned.

"Calm down, Jason; her brother's been very sick," Rick explained. "Look, you take over the accounts till Yvonne returns, and let Rachel deal with the patients. I'll be home in ten days."

Exasperated, Dr. Samuels immediately fell into a deep sleep.

He arrived home on a Sunday, and was surprised that Yvonne didn't answer his frantic texts and email messages. He was sure she'd be at the office on Monday, but still, he was concerned for her welfare.

Jason came to his house before the office opened on Monday and barged through the door.

"Sit down, because we have to talk," he insisted.

"I have spent the past ten days reviewing all the entries and withdrawals for your accounts going back years. It's clear Yvonne created dummy accounts and then siphoned the cash into her own bank. If I were you, Rick, I'd take a hard look at your drug purchases and sales too.

She could have been selling on the side."

Dr. Samuels was dumbfounded. Yvonne, loyal Yvonne, was the worst kind of thief, because he felt he could have trusted her with his life.

"It gets worse, Rick. In the past, she took small sums, but over time, she was much bolder. I'm afraid you're going to have to borrow money in order to keep the practice afloat."

The doctor's face exploded in anger. "And where was my esteemed accountant and why did it take you so long to pick up this larceny?"

"Your memory's short, Rick. Every time I wanted to sit with you to review your accounts, you sent me to Yvonne. You had zero interest in the 'money thing.'"

Dr. Samuel knew Jason was right, yet it was hard to reconcile the Yvonne he had known for so long with the irrefutable evidence Jason had provided.

As difficult as it was, Dr. Samuels called the police and reported a major theft. They located Yvonne, who denied all charges, but she was eventually found guilty and convicted. More drama ensued, as Yvonne attempted suicide. Her attempt failed, as did Dr. Samuels's efforts to reclaim the stolen money, which had all been spent.

The whole experience forced Dr. Samuels to reorganize his office and his attitude toward his finances. Since many of his patients paid cash (they didn't want their spouses to know the source of their "refreshed look"), he divided the financial work. One assistant now opens envelopes and processes payments, while the other takes the cash to the bank.

He also made sure to meet with his accountant on a monthly basis to reconcile statements with his patients' and insurance companies' payments. He learned the hard way that betrayal can land on anyone's doorstep, including his.

Dr. Samuels had blindly trusted his loyal assistant to handle the complex finances of his plastic surgery practice, and had believed in a basic tenet of organizational trust: that employees do not steal from their employers.

Now, Dr. Samuels's new financial system is based on critical checks and balances as well as regular meetings with his staff and accountant. "Trust, but verify" is his new motto.

Wise trust is the third type of trust. As Dr. Steven Stosny explains, "Wise trust assesses the probability of betrayal, in recognition that we are all frail creatures capable of betrayal in weaker moments. Realistically, it's possible that any of us could betray a loved one. Blind trust denies this darker characteristic of human nature; suspiciousness exaggerates it. Wise trust is an assessment that the probability of betrayal is low."[3]

Wise trust can't always save you from betrayal (think back to Ingrid's background check on Andy), but it can protect you from someone's darker side.

Sophia, Ben, and Dr. Samuels trusted, but neglected to verify. They all had pieces of information that should've caused mistrust, but they ignored them. Ingrid thought she had done everything she could to verify, but gave up final control of the verification process. The message is simple: trust wisely, not blindly, always verify, and always trust your gut.

Use wise trust to prepare yourself for the possibility of betrayal or to minimize its impact.

Trust gives us permission to take risks, but if those risks turn out badly, they can chip away at our trust in others. As we have seen, one harmful action can set betrayal in motion and destroy trust.

In the end, trust requires both vulnerability and risk. Because you

---

3   Stosny, "Trust Wisely: Living and Loving after Betrayal."

trust another person, you believe that trust is deserved. This assumption can lead to disappointment, or worse, betrayal.

One of our goals in this book is to help you learn the skills of wise trust so you can protect yourself by safely trusting others.

Yes, betrayal is a reality in life, but it is not the end; it's an unexpected detour on the road to your future. And, as we will see in Chapter Two, there are warnings that can signal trouble on the horizon and warn about that detour coming up ahead.

TAKEAWAYS

1. Wise trust is your new best friend. Reason, facts, and vigilance are required before giving your trust to another.

2. Being betrayed will cause you to ask yourself if you can ever trust people again. Think about what is worse: the prospect of eternal loneliness or taking the risk.

3. Your gut is the best barometer for things that don't seem right. Pay attention, because it's your natural warning system.

4. Friends and business partners make uneasy bedfellows. Be cautious as you move into a professional relationship and maintain a level of caution throughout the relationship.

5. No matter how well you know someone, you may never fully know his or her moral compass.

CHAPTER TWO

Red Flags? What Red Flags? I Never Saw 'Em Coming

We don't see things as they are. We see things as we are.
—Anaïs Nin, *Seduction of the Minotaur*

O h, those little signs of trouble you should have seen, but never did. They're always front and center in every betrayal. So why do we ignore these tiny alarm bells? Because we have a relationship with or loyalty to the person, which enables *betrayal blindness*.

Betrayal occurs when someone intentionally acts in ways that favors their own interest at the expense of another's. The betrayer, feeling superior to the betrayed, sends out ominous signs that let the betrayed know how little their relationship is valued.

Christopher Chabris and Daniel Simons, psychologists and authors of *The Invisible Gorilla,* researched the dangers of focusing only on what one expects to see.[4] Their most famous experiment involved a two-minute video in which two teams, one wearing black shirts, one wearing white, passed a basketball between them.

The audience is told to focus solely on and count the number of passes that the team wearing white makes. In the middle of the video, a person wearing a gorilla suit walks through the middle of the game, stops, beats his chest, and walks on. In the debrief, typically less than 80 percent of the audience sees the gorilla because they are so intent on following the team members in white shirts.

This has a critical application to seeing red flags: if you are not looking for them, and not sensitive to seeing anything that you are *not* looking for, you will miss them.

Understanding this, our survivors might have seen many of the red flags of their potential betrayal flying high. In some cases, they could have predicted betrayal was right around the corner. Instead, they chose to close their eyes to the warnings because they could not believe that a person they trusted would shatter that trust. Just as people do not see the gorilla, our survivors did not see the red flags warning of the oncoming betrayal.

There's a reason betrayal is symbolized as a knife through the heart. It's because it leaves us feeling unsafe, unmoored, diminished, and alone.

Many betrayals take place within a power equation, where the betrayer takes advantage of inequality in the relationship. There's a special language too. How many times have you heard "Trust me"? In certain contexts, it really means "Obey me and ignore my behavior."

While bad behavior may slip into immorality through thought-

---

4   Chabris and Simons, *The Invisible Gorilla.*

lessness or inattention, betrayals are never spontaneous. To be effective, they are carefully planned and executed. And usually, the betrayer drops hints, those red flags, throughout the process.

Mark A. Seabright and Marshall Schminke's research on "Immoral Imagination and Revenge in Organizations" highlights the steps the betrayer must take in order to deliver maximum impact:[5]

1. Identify the desired outcome and goal for the betrayal: "John is the one obstacle to my promotion."

2. Turn off any feelings of empathy for the target of your betrayal: "He doesn't care about me. Why should I care about him?"

3. Dehumanize the target. The target of betrayal is no longer seen as a friend, lover, or colleague, but rather as a target or object that no longer matters: "It's not about John; it's about what's best for me and the company. They need my skills, and he is simply an obstacle."

4. Weigh the alternatives and examine their implications: "No matter what I do or the ways I have tried to get the CEO to notice my contribution, John always seems to block notice of my accomplishments with his own bragging. There is no way to get around him."

5. Consider the impact of actions on the ultimate goal: "If he's that talented, he can always find another job."

6. Think about the effects on the interests of others: "Everyone hates him anyway; he's just self-serving and self-promoting."

---

5   Seabright and Schminke, "Immoral Imagination and Revenge in Organizations: At Our Best: Moral Lives in a Moral Community."

7. Envision the outcome, both in terms of the extent of harm to the betrayed and the benefit to the betrayer in achieving the ultimate goal and desired outcome: "Once I let everyone know that he asked me to keep his secret that he is looking around at bigger opportunities, they will ask him to leave and promote me for my loyalty."

It doesn't matter if the betrayer wants to inflict pain for its own sake, or snatch the golden ring at the expense of another's well-being. In either case, the person who is betrayed is dehumanized into simply a means to a desired end. In this way, the person betrayed is never at fault for the betrayer's decision to betray.

This chapter will focus on stories where the red flags were flying, but remained invisible to those who were about to be betrayed. Red flags take on many different shapes, as you will soon see. Subtle warnings become red flags too late in the game.

A COVER-UP COVERED IN FALSE ASSURANCES

Gina Spero was chair of the audit committee of the board of a publicly traded company.

Her first impression of Jeff, the newly hired and well-known CEO, was that he had an abundance of confidence and experience, and that was exactly what the company needed. But Gina quickly developed a feeling that perhaps his confidence was not very well founded.

"I believe in pushing the envelope around risk in order to maximize growth," he announced at one of his early meetings with the board. "Isn't that what you hired me to do?"

Gina was taken aback by this statement. It was quite an overreach for a new CEO. His subsequent actions further demonstrated that he also believed in maximum media attention for his company, but also for himself.

As he warned in that early board meeting, Jeff pushed the firm into uncharted waters, making large trades significantly above the historical limits. His calls for these big bets rattled many people, including some members of the board.

At one particular meeting, Gina cautioned the board about increasing the positions Jeff and senior management were proposing.

"I know we're on a fast track here, but we've got to be fiscally responsible. I'm casting a 'no' vote," she firmly stated. Since she was chair of the audit committee, the board supported her vote that time.

Jeff flashed her a look that was meant to kill. Gina was getting increasingly uneasy about his integrity and judgment, but she and the board were assured by many experts that sufficient controls were in place to protect the company. The company was in a state of transition, so some risk was warranted, and doing nothing could result in the company's failure.

Deeply concerned, Gina began to think, The emperor has no clothes.

In subsequent board votes, Jeff convinced a majority of the board members that his direction was necessary for the viability of the company, and Gina was outvoted. Soon the large trades caught up with him from a number of perspectives. The company was losing tens of millions of dollars and facing a critical crisis. The regulators and the media were taking note of the large positions and continuing losses of the company. Management was scrambling for a capital infusion that would avoid massive layoffs, as well as searching for a buyer.

A potential sale was now high on the to-do list, but at the last minute, a near-billion-dollar "discrepancy" was discovered in customer funds. How could this have happened? A billion dollars goes missing without someone noticing? There had been so much activity during this period that the system was overloaded, and record keeping was temporar-

ily behind. The answer, many months later, was that also, senior management had misled board members, advisors, and the auditor on the company's liquidity, and the funds were ultimately recovered. But the damage had already been done.

In hindsight, some red flags were obvious early on and others appeared over time. Management knowingly and secretly tried to inflate the company's earning toward the end, as they became increasingly desperate to show a profit. This was caught by Gina and the audit committee. At the behest of the auditors and the company's outside SEC counsel, management was forced to correct the earnings release. An all-nighter of phone calls finally came to an end with a 5:00-a.m. approval of the corrected numbers by the audit committee. If the company hadn't had to declare bankruptcy, an investigation of management's duplicity and culpability would have been the next step.

The press was all over this breach, as was the SEC. Investigations and numerous lawsuits followed, and the independent board was sued for billions of dollars. While insurance covered the directors, it was nowhere close to these amounts. Jeff resigned, as did Gina and the rest of the board.

This was only the beginning of the betrayals.

Because Gina, as audit committee chair, was intimately involved with oversight of the company's finances, she sat in on the preliminary hearing for the lawsuit. She couldn't believe the judge's immediate bias.

In his opening remarks, before one word of testimony had been given, he declared, "This situation is a train wreck. I do not know how the board could be so ignorant."

As the proceeding continued over time, he constantly ruled against the board despite favorable facts and solid legal arguments. Negative news reports seemed to be the basis for his decisions, even though there were many inaccuracies in the press. It was no surprise that Gina and her colleagues did not want this case to go to trial, at least before this judge.

But the pain was not over. Next, as Gina prepared to be a witness for the first trial, she was called for a preliminary conversation with the lawyers.

At last, she hoped, the truth would come out. Hours later, her bubble was burst:

"Ms. Spero, you have given us the clearest and most complete understanding of the events. However, we won't be calling you to testify," they said, shutting down further discussion. "You see, your testimony doesn't fit our narrative."

Obviously, the story had been, and was going to be, written without her voice.

These were very public betrayals—ones that tarnished Gina's hard-earned reputation.

She realized her days as a viable candidate for public-company boards were over, despite her having been vindicated in the various investigatory reports. In addition, the stock she had earned as payment for sitting on the board was now worthless.

A network of good friends stood by Gina and offered her constant, invaluable support. Gina's day-to-day mission became helping employees of the battered company find new positions. She also began to volunteer more and actively mentored others, allowing her to share her skills and experience in other ways. The old axiom that says helping others can help oneself is very true.

Through helping others, she slowly climbed out of her dark hole of embarrassment. Unfortunately, she was never selected as a corporate director again.

Jeff ended up paying, out of his own pocket, a large regulatory fine.

Gina survived, and gained a healthy skepticism for our judiciary and regulatory institutions. She also realized that even when those red flags were waving, it was difficult for board members to comprehend the lengths senior management would go to in order to cover up problems and protect themselves. The board as a whole was assured by management that the extent of the potential damage was limited and controllable. They had never before experienced the combination of negative factors that developed very rapidly. It's a perfect example of the *Invisible Gorilla* study findings: they did not see what they did not expect.

What were the lessons Gina took from this violation of organizational trust? She learned to never blindly accept "trust me" from a new CEO, no matter how good his or her experience appears. Next, she learned to take heed of her uneasiness with a CEO's style and substance or lack thereof—simply put: to trust her gut. And finally, she learned to stay personally engaged in every detail of an investigation, even when standing up to people with more experience and well-regarded reputations. She recognized the need to weigh the risks of acting vs. not acting.

Gina remained involved in the litigation because her reputation was on the line. She learned that "reputational risk" is very real and should not be underestimated. While many people simply stick to "Would you want to see this on the front page of the Wall Street Journal?" as a rule of thumb, Gina advises, "Never do or write anything that you wouldn't want to be questioned about by thirty lawyers in a deposition."

Lastly, Gina learned to keep trusted friends close during complicated times. Not everyone stood by her when the going got really rough, but her true friends did. Because she chose to be active and engaged instead of passive and invisible, she was able to enlist the help of others and welcomed their input. By doing this, she afforded herself permission to listen to the advice of others as she negotiated her next steps. In short, Gina discovered the value of trusting her instincts, reaching out for support, and moving on. Battle scarred but still standing is just fine in the end.

Now see how many red flags you can spot in the next story.

RED FLAG OR STORM WARNING?

Sally's work space was a mess. Protein bar wrappers, empty water bottles, and half-written reports were strewn between notes for marketing presentations. Priscilla knew Sally was scattered. (With two marriages behind her and several children, who wouldn't be?)

But Sally continued to deliver for Priscilla's consultancy firm in a big way. In fact, Sally was her highest paid independent contractor.

The two had met through Matt, a mutual colleague and friend.

"Pris, I think Sally's skills could strengthen your organization and add some revenue," Matt explained when he introduced them.

He was right. In less than three years, Sally billed more than a million dollars through the firm by taking Priscilla's leads and running with them.

But Priscilla thought it was odd that during those years when Sally was billing $40,000 some months, and receiving monthly payouts, she constantly pressed Priscilla for payroll dates. Another disturbing fact was that Sally took the credit for bringing in new clients who had been in the pipeline that Priscilla had developed. Unbeknownst to Priscilla, she constantly bragged to their friend Matt how lucky Priscilla was to have Sally building the business.

"Sally, are you betting heavy in Vegas, or what?" Priscilla joked. They both laughed, and Sally told her she was refinishing her kitchen. "You know, Pris, if these guys don't get paid on time, the family's eating out of the microwave."

Priscilla conveniently swept all these flickering warning signs under the rug until a phone call came in from Andrea, one of Priscilla's clients.

"I'm a little confused," Andrea said. "Why did Sally send me a new contract?"

Equally confused, Priscilla immediately confronted Sally with this information.

"Gosh, I'm sure it's a misunderstanding," Sally replied. "Let me check into how that happened."

But then two more of Priscilla's clients called with the same question. Priscella asked for copies.

Priscilla reviewed the "new contracts" and suddenly the misunderstanding turned out to be an active effort on Sally's part to steal clients from Priscilla's firm. Sally was fired that day.

When Priscilla circled back to Matt, he was horrified, but chalked it up to Sally's midlife crisis.

"Not a crisis, Matt, a full-blown act of self-destruction and betrayal," Priscilla corrected him.

Pricilla's red flags couldn't have been louder or brighter. Under the heading of *That's her style; it's not my style,* Priscilla allowed unusual behavior to continue. Sally's constant need for cash was one red flag. Taking credit for acquiring clients that were given to her by Priscilla was another. Sally's personal life offered still more warnings, as it was littered with two discarded marriages that were caused by Sally's many extramarital affairs; cheating on others was core to Sally's lifestyle.

Priscilla learned the hard way that red flags need to be heeded. As soon as she had doubts about Sally's behavior, her trust needed to be continually verified. While many people get divorces, both of Sally's were based on her affairs with married men. Stealing husbands was the foreshadowing for stealing clients.

By ignoring Priscilla's role in "giving" Sally's clients, Sally acted—as does any betrayer—as if Priscilla was unnecessary to her success. That was Sally's justification of her attempted theft. Here, we see both the mind of the betrayer and the value of paying attention to red flags.

Leslie's story also contains many ignored red flags in a breach of trust by a close friend:

A BFF BETRAYAL

"He's impossible. Just impossible," moaned Leslie who was heavily pregnant with her second child.

Sandra knew all too well the complicated relationship Leslie had with her boss. Even as they both sat in the sun-drenched park, Sandra tried to relieve her friend's stress.

"Leslie, you've got to ease up. You're doing great work despite this guy's antagonism. My God, your responsibility has skyrocketed in the past few years," Sandra said encouragingly.

Leslie never understood why Sandra always flattered her, supported her, and told her how lucky she was to have such a great husband and job. So Leslie shut down her discomfort and accepted the fact Sandra was unilaterally on her side.

"Leslie, all these stories of yours make me happy I blew off the corporate world."

"You don't miss it?" Leslie inquired.

"Not. One. Bit," came Sandra's reply.

That evening, Leslie thought carefully about her run-up to her forth-coming maternity leave. It had been an intense time of planning for a global conference that the company was relying on to fuel increased visibility and sales. And that was in addition to all the other projects she was involved in as the director of marketing. But she had every confidence in her event planner, Neal, who would execute flawlessly during her absence. That was, until Neal told her he was taking another job right away.

"It's my dream, Les, otherwise I'd never leave you in the lurch like this," he said apologetically.

"So, Leslie, what are you going to do about this little hiccup?" her boss asked with the usual snark. "Obviously, the baby's coming soon, and our conference is ten weeks out," he continued. "Awfully bad planning," he said while staring at her stomach with his signature derogatory grin.

"I have got it handled," she smiled back.

And the truth was, she had. As soon as Neal resigned, she called Sandra. Sandra was an experienced event planner who she trusted completely. With a little cajoling and the promise of a short gig, Leslie was sure Sandra would help her out. After all, they had been good friends for so many years, and Sandra had been very supportive of her as she'd described all of her challenges.

Sandra agreed to fill in for Leslie, and when it was finally time for Leslie to take her maternity leave, it worked beautifully. Leslie didn't worry that Sandra never called, trusting that she was merely being a good friend by giving Leslie bonding time with her new baby. Leslie did, however, get calls from her coworkers, who were concerned about Sandra's groveling to the boss. Leslie brushed off their worries by explaining Sandra was doing all she could to make the situation work.

Yet, unbeknownst to Leslie, in her absence, Sandra was working very hard to flatter Leslie's boss and develop a strong relationship with him. She was rebuilding the meticulous event plans from the ground up, focusing on aspects that could put her in the spotlight.

"Not that I want to criticize Leslie's work," Sandra would begin each report to her boss, "but we can do better."

The global conference went off flawlessly, and while telling Leslie about it, Sandra was careful to gloss over the changes she had made. She also "forgot" to mention the praise she'd received from "their" boss.

One week before Leslie was to return from her maternity leave, she was notified that her department was being reorganized. Her role had been redefined in a way that made it a very different job. Perhaps not surprisingly, this new job fit Sandra's skills perfectly. Sandra was offered the new role, which she accepted, and became a permanent hire.

Leslie was blindsided but didn't blame Sandra, because at first, she believed the past animosity with her boss was the real cause. But suddenly, she saw the obvious: Sandra had used knowledge gleaned from their many long conversations about her boss's style and preferences to build a relationship with their boss, destroy Leslie's reputation, and promote her own.

It was a complete betrayal, one that would soon be overtaken by a far more personal one.

As Leslie was dealing with a newborn and a toddler, she was also facing a deteriorating marriage. She felt her husband was verbally and emotionally abusive to her and her children. She and her husband had tried counseling, but the relationship was beyond repair. She decided to move forward with divorce proceedings, charging her husband with abuse. Because of these charges, the judge had ruled that her husband could not visit the children without an impartial third person, but, after negotiations, determined that this person could be of her husband's choosing. Leslie's husband did not tell her the name of this third party before arriving for his first "accompanied" visit.

Leslie will never forget that day. Her husband walked through the door, followed closely by Sandra.

It's a fact of life that all friendships are based on trust. Friends look out for one another's interests, and never take advantage of a confidence for their own self-interest. Long-lasting friendships are based on wise trust. Over the years, there are many opportunities for betrayal, and if they never happen, it appears safe to trust.

By exploiting Leslie's confidences, Sandra inflicted real trauma on her so-called friend in both her personal and professional life. As we've said, betrayers toss compassion and morality out the window. Any shred of empathy for the suffering that will take place is conveniently erased, if it appears at all. And that's the simple answer to the question "How could she?"

Years later, Leslie was successful in shaping a new future. She was divorced, and the founder and CEO of her own business, which she funded with her severance package. Asked about the lessons she learned, Leslie said she should have been more suspicious of Sandra's constant and over-the-top admiration of her life. In retrospect, it seems Sandra simply wanted to take over Leslie's life. And, she also learned, when it comes to parental leave, be careful of dotting all the i's and crossing all the t's. It's important to leave some things undone that require people to call you and reinforce how and why you are missed. If everything left behind is perfect, someone else can easily displace or even *replace* you by taking credit for the work you did. Finally, beware of possible motivations and ambitions when someone is "temporarily" filling in for you.

The next story of organizational betrayal is filled with even more red flags.

THE GREATEST RED FLAG OF ALL:
"I'M ONLY HERE TO HELP"

"It just smells funny," said Evan to Andy, the VP of IT. "I mean, why would we be working on the same initiative as the shared-services team? Why would John, our COO, not want them to know about it?"

"Crazy, right? But John must know what he's doing," replied Andy. "So we carry on. I plan to brief him on a weekly basis about the progress of our work. We just need to trust that it is all about politics, and he knows how to play the game well."

It all started when the parent company wanted to get the subsidiary that Evan and Andy worked for ready for sale. On top of that, parent company's data center was being disbanded and migrating to the cloud. How best to do it was the question. Replication of the existing infrastructure or creating a new one based on the subsidiary's in-house experience? Usually, the parent company's shared services team would cooperate with them, but this was not the path John had chosen.

"That would be too large of a group to get much done," he remarked. "Let's keep it separate, and let's keep it to ourselves."

The work went on for months. To complicate matters further, Stuart, the CEO, engaged an outside consultancy to assist him in the sale of the company. Spoiler alert. The lead consultant was an old and dear friend of Stuart's.

John asked Andy to prepare and present his team's work with the group at a monthly status meeting, where Stuart, John, and executives from the parent company were present.

After Andy's presentation, the silence was deafening.

"How could you keep us out of the loop on this?" demanded Stuart, the CEO. "And correct me if I'm wrong, Andy, but isn't shared services also working on the same initiative? What a stupid duplication of effort, not to mention money! I'm outraged."

41

John, Andy's boss, nodded gravely at Stuart's assessment and made a righteous show of indignant support of Stuart's anger. This was just the first sign of the betrayals to come. Andy knew, but did not say, that John was the one responsible for requesting the presentation, the work plan, and the secrecy surrounding it.

"I'm toast," Andy moaned after the meeting, "completely screwed."

But things were just warming up. After that meeting, CEO Stuart added another challenge to his friend, the consultant.

"Figure out this damn data-migration mess with John. I can't lose any more time on this!" yelled Stuart. John, following orders, immediately told Andy that the consultant was now in charge.

"Andy, why don't you take me through every detail of this?" said the consultant, "Tomorrow I'll have all of my people here."

Andy was a good corporate citizen and worked with his team to prepare a full tutorial, documenting all the systems, processes, and skill sets. After the presentation, he realized that the consultant was pushing his team to present an outsourced migration proposal to be run by the consultant's firm. It was clearly unethical, unprofessional, and irresponsible.

But worse was to follow. Andy's phone rang, and on the other end was a long-standing technology partner who confidentially told him the consultancy had reached out to him. It was something right out of The Godfather.

"Give me a monthly fee, and we'll see the migration business swings to you," the messenger had told the partner.

The partner refused. He knew extortion when he heard it.

Andy reached out to the parent company anonymously. Not wanting to compromise the cloud partner for sharing the information, he felt anonymity was necessary. Despite the anonymity, within a month, Andy was written up for submitting "unapproved" travel expenses to a conference, even though they had been previously approved. Termination *followed. The department was outsourced.*

No action was taken against the consultants, who were seen as super-stars for creating this new cost-saving initiative, nor against John, who was congratulated for stopping the expensive redundancy.

Andy faced a blatant betrayal of organizational trust. Red flags don't get much bigger than being told to head a secret project, a CEO who brings in a "friend" to help "right the ship," and an immediate boss who disavows knowledge of the "secret" project he initiated. By agreeing to keep this team's work a secret from the parent organization, Andy became complicit with the saboteurs. Even worse, as the lowest-level manager in that hierarchy, he was set up to take the fall. It was clearly a case of organizational trust betrayed. Sadly, Andy saw the red flags but ignored his own best judgment and gut reactions, and by doing so, signed his own corporate death warrant.

The next two stories about Jeremy and his two marriages emphasize how important it is to identify red flags, heed them, learn from them, and be prepared to apply that learning to prevent future betrayals.

LOVE IS BLIND

Let's start with wife number one.

Diana was sitting in the witness chair distraught.

"I can't go on," she sobbed.

"I. Simply. Can. Not."

Sympathetic to her extreme distress, the judge called for yet another hour-long delay in Jeremy and Diana's divorce trial.

Jeremy raised his eyebrows, aware that this was quite a performance. He saw the pattern clearly. It was just another round of crying, delaying, and more crying, all in the interest of winning over the court's sympathy for Diana.

With all the evidence Jeremy held against his wife, maybe someone should have been sympathetic to him. After all, she was the one who had pilfered hundreds of thousands of dollars in gold coins from his safe as he campaigned for a seat in Parliament.

The one who'd carried on a secret affair with his—yes, his—lawyer, who was also a longtime friend. At the very least, he could fire his lawyer on the grounds of conflict of interest as well as just basic betrayal!

Diana was also the one who'd claimed the missing candelabras, art, and furniture were being evaluated for insurance, when in fact, she was selling his belongings to the highest bidders and putting the cash in her own safe-deposit box. It was through the work of his second lawyer that they discovered a monthly charge for that box that exposed Diana's chicanery. Note to self: it is always a red flag when valuable objects go missing for a considerable amount of time.

Through it all, Diana had curried favor with Jeremy's friends to gain their loyalty. She'd even bribed his driver to keep tabs on him.

But the strongest evidence Jeremy had was from Basil, the president of the auction house where Diana had sold his family treasures.

When Basil was asked in court if he recognized Diana, he replied yes, he recognized the woman, but not the name. That's because she had sold everything under a false name.

Ultimately, evidence and fact won over sympathy, and the judge ruled Diana was liable for all of Jeremy's legal costs in addition to reimbursement for all of the items that she'd sold.

LOVE IS STILL BLIND

Jeremy was shocked when his second wife, Kate, stormed onto the sixth tee of the golf course, and in front of his foursome, demanded the keys to the car.

Her voice was one decibel below a scream, and Jeremy knew why.

A few days before, he'd overheard a compromising voicemail between Kate and his best friend. Knowing this would be the key to any divorce action, Jeremy locked the audiotape in his briefcase in the trunk of the car. Sadly, Jeremy has luck with neither wives nor friends.

But this was only the beginning of the ongoing betrayals in Jeremy's divorce case with Kate.

While he was traveling on business, she emptied the house, took everything but one bed, a few dishes and a lamp. Of course, she grabbed the car and pocketed the tax returns, but what threw him completely was that she took Barney, his ten-year-old dog. Barney had been part of Jeremy's life long before Kate had ever entered the scene. It was unbearably cruel. He didn't miss Kate; he missed Barney.

Kate wanted half his pension. She even wanted Jeremy to write a letter of support when she was accused of cheating in golf at the club.

When Jeremy finally took Kate to court, she admitted Barney was his dog. The judge made her liable for Jeremy's legal fees and she immediately had to return Barney to his rightful owner. She was required to give back his furnishings too.

While Jeremy was great at seeing red flags, he didn't use them to avoid betrayal. He sadly admits that when he's in love, he trusts. Totally, completely, and blindly. Then he marries, and inevitably, he is betrayed. When asked about this blind spot, Jeremy answered that he couldn't live in a world without trust ... or without love. For Jeremy, love and trust are the same. In that case, he should *always trust and always verify*. Jeremy needs to keep a sign on his mirror that says "wise trust or no trust."

The people in each of these narratives "just knew" something wasn't right. They felt it and sensed it, but chose to ignore the signs. Why? Blame blind trust and don't forget the influential role personal relationships play in this game. As Scottish theologian Kay Carmichael noted, betrayal is the "shadow companion of trust." It can live quietly below the surface waiting for the right moment to strike. And the more blindly we trust, the easier we make it for the right moment to occur.

To summarize Joshua Coleman, co-chair of the Council on Contemporary Families and a psychologist with a private practice, because we trust, we waive disbelief. And when we waive disbelief, we ignore red flags. And that's why betrayal is so traumatizing. It does more than challenge our world order; it smashes it to bits.

This feeling of trauma and dislocation when our world is smashed to bits is perfectly described in this excerpt from a New York Times review of the last episode of the long-running TV series *The Americans*. Here, Stan, the American FBI officer who has become best friends with the covert Russian spy family, learns of their betrayal of his trust. As Margaret Lyons, the reviewer, describes, Stan knows that "death isn't always a punishment, and it certainly isn't the harshest one. The rending of one's identity—not being able to be who you were before, to know who you knew, to love who you loved, to trust your own thoughts, to have a cohesive and continuing story of yourself—creates a permanent wound."[6]

In every relationship, any behavior that doesn't make sense may be a red flag. Some are subtle and others are flagrant. Instinct alerts us to these warnings with a twinge or a "Gosh, that's strange," because

---

6   Poniewozik, Hale, and Lyons, "The Best TV Episodes of 2018."

our subconscious is always at work. And the subconscious sees and understands things before they hit conscious awareness. Some call these red flags "gut feelings." We sense something is amiss, but we may not know—or want to know—what it is. These red flags are brushed aside, because we see things as we want to see them.

Carly Simon and Jacob Brackman fully captured the nature of red flags in a relationship with the song "It's Not Like Him":

When Tom came home his hair was combed
He bought snakeskin boots in Rome
That's not like him ...

I caught a glimpse of Tom today
At a checkout counter, about to pay
He had a girl on his arm
I'm glad he's helping out the poor
It's not like the Tom I knew before
Something so touching it made me cry
But my heart was racing, I don't know why

Of course, we can't live our lives filled with suspicion, but consider replacing "blind trust" with "wise trust." It's not distrust, but a willingness to look beyond the superficial and take notice of any requests that don't make sense. In her excellent book, *Willful Blindness: Why We Ignore the Obvious at Our Peril,* author Margaret Heffernan discusses the legal principle of whether someone can be held responsible for not knowing a fact.[7] She notes that a defendant must be seen as having knowledge of something if he "willfully blinded himself to its existence." She further quotes Judge Simon Lake that "You are responsible if you could have known, would have known, and should have known something which instead you endeavored not to see."

---

7   Heffernan, *Willful Blindness: Why We Ignore the Obvious at our Peril.*

In relationships, no one wants to look for problems, but red flags are a sign that something may be wrong. They are a universal symbol of distress. As Alicia H. Clark, psychologist and anxiety expert, wisely noted in her book *Hack Your Anxiety: How to Make Anxiety Work for You in Life, Love, and All That You Do*, "Anxiety is not a noise (Cover your ears!), but rather a signal (Look over here!) ... Our anxiety manifests as something unpleasant, but it is trying to protect us, motivate us, and educate us ... Understanding that anxiety holds the seeds of growth can help develop an attitude of curiosity and cultivate a more conscious experience of it."[8]

Feeling anxious about something without being able to name it may well be the first red flag. To identify red flags, listen to your subconscious and your intuition, and name the sources of your stress. All this really requires is bringing your prior experience to bear in your current situation. All of us have a small internal monitor that can be useful if only we take the time to listen. Create the time for a gut check. It works like this:

1. Give yourself a quiet space to reflect.

2. Listen to your inner voice. Are you uncomfortable? Anxious? Stressed?

3. Think about other times you have had these feelings— anxiety, anger, sadness, etc. What was happening then? Were you at risk of betrayal? Were you betrayed?

4. What have you done when you've had these feelings in the past? Did it work? If yes, how; if no, why?

5. Allow yourself to question the individual's behavior. Does it make sense? Is it consistent with past behavior? Is something

---

8   Clark, *Hack Your Anxiety: How to Make Anxiety Work for You in Life, Love, and All That You Do*

very different going on? Is it "not like" him or her?

6. Are you blaming yourself for another person's faults and bad behavior? Are you really to blame?

7. Think about all the times you've listed to your gut and it helped. How can it help now?

8. What is your gut telling you?

The value of the gut check, and listening to one's intuition is not new. In the seventeenth century, the French mathematician, philosopher, and theologian Blaise Pascal recognized that truth is accessible in two ways: via the heart and via the mind.[9] What he calls the heart is intuition. It is closely connected to the body, and includes everything we instinctually understand. He explains that the mind, however, can only infer from data and observation.

He writes, "The heart has its reasons, which reason does not know ... Reasons come to me afterwards, but at first a thing pleases or shocks me without my knowing the reason, and yet it shocks me for that reason which I only discover afterwards."

That was Pascal's gut talking loud and clear, and his mind playing catch-up.

So you've seen red flags, you realize that your relationship is based on blind trust, and your gut is yelling, "Betrayal ahead!!" Now what?

---

9   Pascal, *Thoughts.*

TAKEAWAYS

1. If you feel uncomfortable and stressed, always perform the gut check described previously.

2. Use your anxiety as energy to identify the source and address the challenge.

3. Think of past "trust your gut" successes. What made them successful? What lessons can you apply to this situation?

4. Ask as many questions as necessary to ensure that your understanding of the situation is crystal clear.

5. Use your intuition and life experiences to help you identify an approach that has succeeded in the past.

6. Act quickly and lock down everything that might be at risk.

7. Avoid the temptation to tell anyone anything until you can distinguish your friends from your enemies. This is the time for wise trust. You can only trust if you continually verify.

8. Remember, only *you* can protect your reputation; don't trust others who say, "Don't worry. You'll be fine." If it doesn't feel fine, it isn't fine.

9. Ensure that you *never* believe that you deserve to be treated badly.

10. Realize that there are no limits to what others might do if their future is at risk. If you sense trouble

brewing, do everything in your power stop it from happening.

11. Recognize that sometimes you will miss the red flags. They may be too subtle. It's not your fault. Do not beat yourself up.

CHAPTER THREE

Betrayed? Never Surrender Your Power or Your Soul

*It's only when the tide goes out that you
learn who was swimming naked.*
—Warren Buffet

T he moment of betrayal is a firm, fast punch to your midsection. It leaves you gasping for a breath of fresh air and stops you in your tracks. This is a physical reaction second to none and what comes next depends on how you react.

Response to a betrayal depends on a great number of factors. Age, gender, cultural variables, history of past trauma, family origins, and spiritual beliefs are but a few.

Extensive clinical research by therapists John Haney and Leslie

Hardie describes three critical steps in the first stage of this gut-wrenching discovery:[10]

1.   Threat Containment

2.   Safety

3.   Self-Care

They all require that you put yourself first, and in this chapter, we will show you how.

When a betrayal rears its ugly head, your fight-or-flight mechanism goes into in full swing Psychologists Jill Duba Sauerheber and J. Graham Disque, academicians and family therapists, paint this picture of that traumatic moment:

"You are in a building and the fire alarm starts going off. You exit the building, the fire department comes, and they turn off the alarms and clear the building for reentry. Now imagine you the left the building, but the fire department never comes. You go back into the building, with the alarm still going off and the strobe lights still flashing. This is how going back into the relationship is for the traumatized betrayed partner. She will reenter without getting the 'all clear,' and yet her response system is still going off."[11]

Understand that every betrayer is a robber. He/she wants to steal your self-esteem and hijack your personal power. In the process of betrayal, the goal is to dehumanize the target before moving in for the kill.

Or, as Professor Howard F. Stein, an organizational anthropologist, has noted in his article "Organizational Euphemism and the Cultural Mystification of Evil," the goal is to "murder the spirit"

---

10   Haney, "Psychotherapeutic Considerations for Working With Betrayed Spouses: A Four-Task Recovery Model."

11   Sauerherber, "A Trauma-Based Physiological Approach: Helping Betrayed Partners Heal from Marital Infidelity."

because the betrayer is enacting a clever form of "human sacrifice" motivated both consciously and unconsciously to undermine and destroy the dignity and humanity of the other.[12]

The betrayer is in full heist mode. That's the power play and the ultimate goal. To keep the betrayer from achieving his/her ends, it's critical to tap into your inner strength. Build it. Nurture it. And keep that steel-like force ready for the onslaught of attack. This is not about you. No one causes another person to betray them. Your only job is to stand strong against the attack.

Despite the initial trauma of the betrayal moment, each of the betrayed in the following stories calls on their inner strength to find a level of control and reverse the power dynamic. In other words, the betrayer did not succeed in destroying them.

In Ellie's story, she dealt with a prolonged betrayal that was driven by a long list of employees, peers, bosses, and lawyers.

REFUSING TO BE THE SCAPEGOAT

The head of the company's internal treasury investigation looked at her hard, and simply said, "Ellie, you've been mugged."

Eleanor Woodward, CEO of a successful US financial services company took a minute before she dared ask the next question.

"How much are we talking, Seth?"

"Hundreds of millions in losses," he replied.

Ellie took off her glasses and fell back into her chair. It was a staggering sum.

After delivering two consecutive years of double-digit growth for the firm, how could something like this happen on her watch? Why weren't these bogus FX trades detected? How had they slipped past the auditors

---

12 Stein, "Organizational Euphemism and the Cultural Mystification of Evil."

and regulators and all those state-of-the-art controls?

The day she was alerted by the head of risk management and chief legal officer, she knew it was a serious situation. But now, for the first time, a price tag was put on the fraud.

Andrew Ansel, a currency trader was responsible for this sophisticated caper that could have decimated the company and ruined livelihoods.

Andrew reported to the head of a fledgling trading unit that was an island unto itself. This unit was not a core business and Ellie had questioned the reason for its creation when she first stepped into the role of CEO. But her board had pushed back, saying they wanted and needed to establish this sector.

As Andrew became a fixture in currency trading, he assumed an arrogance and a Wall Street swagger his boss encouraged. He was bright, and had a firm grasp of the bank's systems and procedures. Later, Ellie learned that he intimidated and ignored other employees who questioned his risky moves.

All of this was on her mind as Ellie mobilized her management team to deal with the monumental crisis at hand. Within forty-eight hours, the conference rooms were overflowing with auditors, analysts, and senior executives. By day three, Ellie was ready to announce publicly the extent of the loss.

Believing transparency was the best course of action, Ellie communicated up and down the ranks to all the stakeholders.

Of course, the press was all over the scandal. The FBI had been called in to investigate Andrew's whereabouts. Ever the manipulator, Andrew was in hiding. The collateral damage was spread far and wide. The company was bracing itself for a decrease in valuation. Reputations were erased, and long-standing employees, fired.

As Ellie put together a timeline for the fraud, and a complete understanding of how the controls were breached, she was battered in the press.

Her phalanx of lawyers claimed they were in her corner. She was not to speak to anyone in the media until her board had approved a public-relations strategy.

"But we need a response; we need to control the messaging right now!" she countered.

"We're working on it," the high-powered legal team replied.

Those above Ellie decreed that "No comment" was, in fact, the only comment that would save the integrity of the organization. Ellie believed that "No comment" would instead destroy the integrity of the organization. Sadly, "No comment" from the credible sources meant the press went elsewhere and created their own very negative and damning version of the facts. After all, as Ellie knew well, in the absence of information, people create their own theories.

Suddenly, former execs who had wanted her job created a campaign to imply she should have known about the rogue trader. Their intention? Make Ellie the scapegoat. How did they do this? Through leaks to the press.

But she refused to go quietly. She would not be scapegoated for a problem she did not create. This betrayal was aimed at her reputation, and she was in battle mode to protect it. Her conversation with her board was a simple one:

"I'm on to what you're doing," she said calmly, "and I'm not afraid to tell the press, the shareholders, and everyone in the industry who it was that insisted on these business activities. And who insisted on providing the oversight that completely missed the fraudulent activity. I've got proof. I refuse to be the scapegoat."

Her strength resulted in her victory. A flurry of management terminations followed, but Ellie was not one of them. She dealt with the painful details of the failed systems and controls as she put new ones in place.

Ellie was keenly aware that her attitude and demeanor would send a critical signal to all those who worked for her. And her innate sense of fairness would not let her walk away from this mess.

Ellie stabilized the company with her key team and left the company once she was convinced her work was done.

As testament to her courage and her contribution to the company's ongoing viability, she was recruited for another CEO position.

In the face of total organizational betrayal, Ellie maintained a firm grasp of her end game and self-esteem. Even though she was attacked, badly bruised, undermined, marginalized, and silenced, Ellie disabled those who wanted to steal her power and control. She knew that strong leaders don't fold when the world around them is in tatters.

Most importantly, she learned never to let an individual or institution control your narrative, because it's your reputation that's at stake. And that means everything for your future.

Another example of hanging tough in the face of the betrayal of organizational trust is Rachel's story. It also illustrates the basic psychological contract between colleagues, especially when there is a power dynamic in play.

STARING DOWN THE BARREL
OF BETRAYAL

Rachel never saw it coming.

As a major buyer for a department store, she always followed company policy by getting her vice president's approval on her orders.

This time was different.

She entered his office with a sheaf of papers for his sign-off.

He put his hand on them and pushed them back toward her.

"I'm not approving them, Red," he said provocatively.

God, how she hated the nickname he had given her.

"Stop it, Simon; you know you verbally approved the orders and they are ready to be shipped," she said.

"Tell ya what: if you want my signature on all of these," he smiled seductively, "let's take that business trip to New York City next month. A nice little dinner followed by a night in my hotel room, and you'll get all the approvals you want."

This was something out of Mad Men—*the quintessential #MeToo moment. Rachel knew she had to act quickly and take control. She didn't want to lose her job, and she certainly didn't want to agree to his grimy proposition.*

She stared him straight in the eyes and simply, firmly said, "No." She then threw all the orders in the trash can and headed back to her office.

As she sat there trying to calm down and determine her next move, the phone rang. It was the VP's assistant, who told her the approvals for her orders had been okayed.

After that, Rachel never again entered the VP's office, and instead channeled everything through his assistant.

Both Ellie's and Rachel's endings proved to be positive ones because each woman was resolute while staring down the barrel of betrayal of organizational trust. Yes, they were facing career-ending situations, but they refused to let the betrayer steal their power and self-esteem. In doing so, they won both the short- and long-term game.

Nicholas's story and his reaction provide a different perspective on organizational trust and the impact of betrayal. Through his ordeal, he gained valuable insights into the nature of leadership, and realized he owned some of the culpability in his betrayal by his employees.

ROBBING A COMPANY AND A SOUL

Nicholas adjusted his chair, turned his face toward the sun, and felt the mountain air fill his lungs. Even with a month of rest, a decent diet, and the weight of his business debacle finally off his shoulders, he felt a deep sadness.

It wasn't supposed to be this way.

Three years ago, Nicholas had built a digital agency from the ground up. It was exciting to create a business with such a hip culture of young designers and content writers. The small group of ten employees was tight-knit, and Nicholas prided himself on the trusted family he had put together.

As the founder and a managing partner, Nicholas was on a punishing schedule to grow the business while keeping current clients happy, and to also manage his growing team. It took energy, focus, and determination. And there was not one detail Nicholas left to chance.

Luckily, Nicholas had two superstars in Geoff and Emma. Emma was the strongest designer in the agency and Geoff an excellent account manager. Together, they made a successful team. While Nicholas felt comfortable with their judgment and skills, he kept a close eye on every aspect of their work. After all, it was his business, and they were still learning.

When everything seemed to be in place, Nicholas decided to take a well-deserved holiday. But not before preparing a highly-detailed status document containing instructions for every possible eventuality. Yes, Nicholas could be obsessive, but every contract he filled and every website he created kept the doors of the agency open and people employed.

When Nicholas returned from his holiday, refreshed and optimistic, Geoff and Emma met him at the front entrance.

"We've got to talk to you," Geoff said with excitement.

"We've got this idea," Emma chimed in.

"Give me time to get settled in my office," Nicholas answered.

But they followed him down the hall and into his office.

"What's this idea?" Nicholas asked, thinking it was a new way to think through website builds.

Geoff beamed with pride and said, "Emma and I are going to form a new company. It'll be so cool. But we're totally going to stay till the end of month for continuity. And we really appreciate all you have done for us."

Remaining calm, Nicholas inquired if they had any clients lined up for their new venture.

"Of course we do," Geoff replied. He then proceeded to list five clients that were currently housed in the agency—five clients that represented 80 percent of the revenue.

Nicholas felt his heart drop to his knees. He was angry and in shock. He thought, I need to stay in control. *But he quickly concluded,* I have no control over anything other than myself.

This was a serious betrayal. Not only had he trusted these two people, but also, he had given them a real opportunity to gain confidence in their skills. And now they were repaying him by threatening the financial viability of the business he had so diligently built.

With as much dignity as he could muster, he asked Geoff and Emma to take the rest of the day off and come see him in the morning.

Nicholas called his lawyers for advice. When they asked for Geoff's and Emma's employee contracts, he discovered they were missing from the files. In his constant focus on the business, Nicholas had neglected to send the lawyers copies. And he realized with a sinking heart that the contracts would not have mattered anyway. He had never included non-solicitation and non-compete clauses in them, as he had felt they would show a lack of trust on his part. A lawsuit became impossible.

In the weeks that followed, Nicholas discovered Geoff and Emma's plans were an open secret with his other employees, contractors, and clients. Not one person had come to Nicholas.

Inevitably, the agency had to shut its doors. People had to find new jobs. All of Nicholas's achievements were erased.

Geoff and Emma's venture lasted six months.

Nicholas describes how he first reacted to the betrayal, and upon reflection, what he learned from this numbing experience:

"At the moment Geoff listed the clients, I was in shock. Deep down, I was devastated and suddenly extremely insecure. My thought was, *It's over. After three years of sixteen-hour days, I have achieved nothing. I will have nothing to show for this.* As soon as I was alone, I broke down in tears."

The worst part of this whole situation? According to Nicholas, "It wasn't that most of the people whom I cared about knew and hadn't defended me. It wasn't that I had somehow lost an entire company. The worst part was that I had let a beautiful relationship come to an end because I had been so dedicated to making the company work. And now, I felt empty and worthless and disgusted with myself."

Despite Nicholas's decision to close down the company, he was able to respond to this "knife to the heart" betrayal with dignity. Although Geoff and Emma had violated his trust, he realized that they were not evil. Instead, Nicholas used the next few months to do some soul searching, asking himself why he had believed the company was one happy family, and what would have been necessary to prevent the betrayal from occurring.

Nicholas was a victim of blind trust coupled with organizational trust. By neglecting the employment contracts, he failed to protect the company. He believed that, as the "boss," he was entitled to total control over "his" people and "his" business.

In hindsight, he realized that his need for oversight of every detail, no matter how trivial, prevented anyone else from feeling accountable or even realizing their own importance to the business. He learned total control is an impossibility, because people will always discover workarounds from feeling controlled.

Nicholas also learned that sharing responsibility gives people a path to success. If they have the space and authority to achieve their goals, their need to go elsewhere is diminished. After better understanding this, Nicholas decided to enroll in an MBA program to expand his leadership capabilities.

John Mark Haney and Liz Hardie's research puts Nicholas's reaction in a common context:

"A betrayed person suffers extreme emotional upheaval marked by rapid fluctuations between hopelessness and despair. Those who are betrayed are not well served and not capable of rushing to a decision about long-term aspects of their life. They need time and support to work through their emotions and learn all the relevant factors necessary to move forward."[13]

Next is Liz's story, which shows how a calm, unemotional reaction at the moment of betrayal can be beneficial.

BETRAYED? STAY COOL

It was the selfie seen round their close-knit community.

How stupid was her husband's mistress to share a photo of the two of them at a New England spa with all of her Facebook friends? And really? A couple's massage?!

So that had been George's true destination this past weekend—not the executive retreat he'd described to her, rudely dismissing all of her questions.

To make things even worse, George's new lady was the wealthy woman who lived across the street. (George had always been attracted to

---

13 Haney, "Psychotherapeutic Considerations for Working With Betrayed Spouses: A Four-Task Recovery Model."

money and the easy life it could buy.)

Liz picked up her cell and told her friends what was happening. Of course, many of them had already seen the post.

"I'm in awe," she told them, "of his classic need to feed his forty-year-old ego."

The next call Liz made was to her mother-in-law, who she truly liked and who, she believed, truly liked her. She explained that George was off with another woman, and the mortifying way she had learned of his betrayal.

Her mother-in-law said quietly, "Liz, it's been forty years to the day since I had to make this same call to my mother-in-law. Do you think it's genetic? How can I help you?"

Hurt and angry, Liz awaited George's return.

He casually walked through the door and asked if dinner was ready.

"You're toast, George; it's all over the internet," Liz said calmly.

"I figured as much. But calm down. I don't want your temper to get the best of you."

Not exactly contrition, *Liz thought. But she brushed aside her anger and asked a serious question that would have consequences for her and their three children.*

"Do we work this out, George?" she asked plainly and calmly.

He paused for an uncomfortably long time. That pause was enough to make her realize he'd mentally moved on. Yet still, he refused to move out during the divorce process, which made life unsettling for everyone.

George's devotion to their neighbor evaporated soon after he met an even wealthier woman in the area.

Now driving an expensive sports car, he parks his new toy in front of his previous girlfriend's house as if to say, "I've got even more perks now."

In pursuit of success, some men climb the corporate ladder; others count on a series of wealthy women.

Liz is happily raising her children as a single mom with the full support of her mother-in-law.

By remaining calm and composed when her husband came home, Liz protected her self-esteem. She allowed herself to move forward with a minimum of visible stress. She firmly understood she had been betrayed, but never relinquished the reins of power to George. In many ways, the very public betrayal helped her. Friends provided immediate support, so she didn't have to worry about what she would say to people.

It was also smart of Liz to reach out to her mother-in-law before her husband told his side of the story. Her mother's-in-law's immediate sympathy helped her stay strong, as did the support of her friends and family. Liz's story shows that you shouldn't be ashamed of sharing your story, because you can be pleasantly surprised at who will step up to support you. Despite what many people think, betrayal is shameful for the betrayer, not the betrayed.

In our next story, Kerry's moment of betrayal helped her to assess her lifetime goals.

WHOSE LIFE IS THIS ANYWAY?

Kerry and her husband, Jay, were a matched set, a perfect pair. They even shared parallel careers in the same industry. Both had an international bent, which meant they loved their postings in Europe. It was exciting raising a family together, working in a variety of foreign countries, and supporting each other in their career aspirations.

After the birth of their second child, Kerry felt it was time to hit the pause button. She wanted to stay at home with her babies for just a year or two, and Jay agreed with her plan. After all, she wasn't giving up on working, just giving herself sometime to be a devoted mom. This is why, during her two-year absence, Kerry made sure she maintained her business relationships, continued to grow her professional network, and even developed new opportunities by doing part-time consulting.

Building and maintaining relationships was Kerry's strength and the reason she was promoted so quickly in her career. So when Jay was up for a senior position in the same company where she was on maternity leave, and needed her contacts to support his candidacy, she brought to bear all her carefully nurtured business relationships.

One in particular, David, could help smooth the way for Jay to get this important job.

"David, I want to ask you a favor that would mean a lot to me."

She explained that Jay was up for regional head and needed relevant info and an introduction or two.

"Happy to do so," David responded. "It's the least I can do after all you've done for me."

Needless to say, Kerry was thrilled when David delivered and Jay was hired. It was a huge step up for Jay in status. And truth be told, it wouldn't have happened without Kerry, because Jay had not developed many solid business connections, let alone deep relationships. That was his blind side.

A year later, Kerry saw an annual self-evaluation lying on Jay's desk. She picked it up and read it out of curiosity. Her curiosity soon turned to shock and anger as she discovered Jay had taken full credit for the "door-opening" relationship with David that was critical to Jay's success.

He had written a self-evaluation that described in detail all the work that she had done, creating a false story about his actions and outcomes. While Kerry did not expect him to say that she had done all this, she was blindsided by his hijacking of her work.

Even more amazingly, he took credit for the relationship building Kerry *was doing during her maternity leave. He described her private meetings with movers and shakers, making it sound as if he were the highly-connected person, not Kerry. And never once did he ask her for permission.*

This was a double betrayal. Jay had stripped Kerry of her belief in their strong marital partnership. By taking credit for her business connections, he'd vaporized what she had done to keep herself relevant in the workplace.

In this document, Jay had revealed himself to be insecure and jealous of her career. Their partnership had morphed into a rivalry.

Kerry was speechless, and chose to remain so. She also chose to never again share work-based information with her husband.

But why?

This all took place decades ago, and Kerry has never confronted Jay about the evaluation. She kept quiet, kept her powder dry, and chose a Zen-like path because all along, Kerry had sensed she was the stronger person. Confrontation would've only served to humiliate her husband and destroy the marriage, something Kerry hadn't wanted to do at that time. Her moment of betrayal led to a critical evaluation of what she wanted from life.

Kerry deftly put aside her emotions to analyze what her next steps should be. She coolly weighed potential outcomes of leaving the marriage, and decided, despite the betrayal of her trust, she would not confront Jay.

Kerry put it best: "I knew that a direct confrontation would probably lead to his humiliation, and he was too proud to live with the knowledge that I had humiliated him. That, in turn, would lead to a divorce. We had two young children and I had no intention of becoming a single parent. So I decided that I would tuck this away in the back of my mind until I decided whether or not I wanted to consider the possibility of divorce. Now that I'm at the end of my career, I am reexamining that question."

Kerry is a shining example of "strategic patience." She weighed her alternatives and chose a path that met her needs. She decided it was better to wait, knowing she was not prepared to open the door to a solution that was not in her best interest.

Kerry shared the words of Don Miguel Ruiz, Mexican author of Toltec spiritualist and neoshamanistic texts and author of *The Four Agreements*, that helped her through her husband's betrayal of her trust in the truthfulness and partnership of their marriage.[14] In parentheses, we have adapted his advice.

1. Be impeccable with your word. *(Do not say things you will later regret.)*

2. Don't take anything personally. *(You are not to blame.)*

3. Don't make assumptions. *(Don't assume others' motivations.)*

4. Always do your best. *(Do not let the actions of others cause you to act poorly.)*

The moment of betrayal demands inner resources and superhero strength. It requires keen analytical skills to evaluate the situation without involving emotion. Cool analysis can preserve your self-esteem and help you maintain control. This is the common thread of all the previous stories, and the key to why the betrayers were not able to steal the power of those they betrayed.

Recognizing how you might respond to a betrayal can help you recover. It is critical that you recognize that what you are feeling is completely normal. To demonstrate the wide range of immediate reactions, Stanley Rachman, a psychologist, researcher, and author of

---

14 Ruiz, *The Four Agreements*.

the research paper "Betrayal: A Psychological Analysis," provides an extensive list, which we have again adapted here:[15]

1. PTSD-like symptoms (Yes, a bomb did go off, a psychological one).

2. Rumination (Thinking about it over and over, and again and again).

3. Hyperarousal (Everything—no matter how trivial—is a threat).

4. Numbing ("This is not happening").

5. Avoidance ("I'll think about it tomorrow").

6. Constant replaying of the event and its meaning (Spending every waking minute obsessing over the details and thinking about all the "if only" scenarios).

7. Worthlessness ("Stupid me; it's my fault").

8. Embarrassment ("I'm going to hide away forever").

9. Loss of self-esteem ("It's no use; I can never succeed again"). And sense of being violated ("How could he/she/the corporation/the lawyer?").

10. Degradation ("It's all over; everyone knows I am ruined").

11. Humiliation ("People are laughing at me").

Keeping an objective appraisal of the betrayal and the outcome is essential. If you blow the event out of proportion, exaggerating its impact on all aspects of your life, you'll only postpone your recovery. The same is true for denying your feelings of anger and hurt. This, too, will delay moving forward.

---

15 Rachman, "Betrayal: A Psychological Analysis."

TAKEAWAYS

Remember, controlling your narrative and keeping your power prevents the betrayer from having power over you.

1. Understand that initially, "a rage so dark and ferocious it scares you," is normal and necessary. —Abigail Trafford, author of *Crazy Time: Surviving Divorce and Building a New Life*[16]

2. Observe the moment of betrayal in third person, taking in your thoughts, feelings, and perceptions.

3. Describe what happened. Write down your feelings. Compose a letter, email, or text, but keep it to yourself.

4. Be aware and act deliberately and thoughtfully. Your radar should be on high alert. Now it's time to be hyper-vigilant and protect yourself above all else.

5. Avoid the temptation to judge yourself and become stuck in a state of recrimination.

6. Assume you've done all the right things and betrayal is still unpreventable, so ease up on yourself. The key to moving forward is self-compassion.

7. Stay connected to others because it can level-set the trauma and increase your resilience.

8. Get yourself to a safe space, both physically and emotionally. Right now, get eight hours of sleep.

---

16 Trafford, *Crazy Time: Surviving Divorce and Building a New Life.*

Being rested will help you think clearly and you're going to need your wits to survive.

9. Don't quit when you're mad. Even if others have the upper hand, circumstances can change in a flash.

10. In a business betrayal, as well as a romantic one, never lose sight of the money. Don't let feelings of friendship or love intrude. Instead, focus on what can be a big help to your future—it's called *cash*.

11. Hold on to your circle of trusted friends and advisors. They can keep you grounded during all the emotional turbulence. They will help you recapture your self-esteem.

12. Do not allow anyone to make you the scapegoat. Defend yourself with documentation. Threats are also an option: "Tell the truth, or I'll go to the press." Get legal support for your situation ASAP. Understand the risk of your actions and the risk of doing nothing.

CHAPTER FOUR

The Family Business: A Hotbed of Betrayal

It's hard to find a good egg in a broken nest.
—Anonymous

I n our interviews, we heard many stories of betrayal within a family business. At first, we categorized them as violations of organizational trust, but then realized a family business is a very different animal. It has a unique cast of characters and a deep emotional past. Because it is a "family," there's an assumption that self-interest plays no part in the decision-making. It's assumed that the "good of the family and the good of the business" take top billing, and all members share the same goals and values. But that's not so, which is why these stories of betrayal deserve their own chapter—

and the betrayers, their own place in hell.

The family business can be a cauldron of backstabbing, fraught with past grievances, sibling rivalry, and high-wire tensions. Imagine these emotions in the context of all the decisions a business makes regarding leadership, finances, and future business direction.

Marcy Syms grew up in, and ultimately sold, her family business. She established, with her father, in his name, the Sy Syms School of Business at Yeshiva University, which focuses on ethical behavior. Marcy wisely notes that one should never confuse childhood fantasies and career realities. Businesses that function like families will not survive. All successful businesses are meritocracies by necessity, and all successful families are bound by unconditional love for each other.

Betrayal in a family business has the potential to destroy both the company and the family itself.

Harry Levinson, a corporate psychologist and family business advisor, raises a warning that unless families face up to and directly address feelings of hostility, the business will suffer and perhaps die.

Bolstering the importance of Levinson's warning, Family Business Institute, in their January 2018 white paper titled "Family Business Succession Planning," note the following:

> 88% of current family business owners believe the same family or families will control their business in five years, but succession statistics undermine this belief. According to The Family Firm Institute, only about 30% of family and businesses survive into the second generation, 12% are still viable into the third generation, and only about 3% of all family businesses operate into the fourth generation or beyond.[17]

Now, add the possibility of betrayal into this equation, and the

---

17 Family Business Institute, "Family Business Succession Planning."

odds for the survival of a family business is even less likely.

Carlos' story is full of the dark alleys a family business can run into.

BLOOD IS NOT ALWAYS THICKER THAN WATER

As the administrative council convened for their weekly meeting, everyone was chatting about their weekend before digging into the agenda. The group included the top echelon: the president, the CFO, the COO, the vice president, the general manager, and Carlos, and the corporate secretary—but today, Mauricio, the CEO, would not be joining them.

Although only twenty-nine years old, Carlos was proud of his track record at one of the largest private mining companies in Latin America. This was a multigenerational family business, and the family controlled 80 percent of the enterprise. Carlos was heavily involved with the technology systems, finding ways to improve them and streamline costs. His diligence paid off when he was asked to join the council as secretary.

The mining company was facing a host of issues, not the least of which was its accelerated growth, which was causing a shortage of reserves.

But Carlos was fully prepared for today's important discussion. He had brought in a Spanish bank to perform a strategic due-diligence process that would help provide a selection of options to solve the company's financial problem. The bank would advise them on which option would be most effective: going public, selling the company, or finding new investors. Carlos was certain the council would be pleased with his update. It was too bad that Mauricio wasn't there to hear the details, but Carlos had promised Mauricio that he would provide a personal debrief once he returned from his outside meetings.

Carlos presented with passion and a clear path for implementation for each of the options.

As he finished, Juan, the executive vice president, looked at his cell phone and declared, "I'm sorry, Carlos, but none of it is feasible. Would you gentlemen excuse me? I'll be right back."

Carlos bubbled with fury at being so rudely cut off.

A moment later, Juan returned with a stranger.

"I'm here to announce," Juan said. "That the company was sold late last night. The deal has just been finalized. Mr. Ortega here, is one of a group of lawyers who purchased it. Shall we all welcome him?"

Carlos felt that the floor had opened and he'd fallen into a pit of alligators.

The group of lawyers who had bought the company were known for their questionable business practices, not to mention their tendency to bleed their acquisitions of value and declare bankruptcy in the end.

If only he had known, Carlos could have saved the company in a way that continued the legacy. But everyone was in the dark, from senior management to the employees.

And who was the person responsible for this bitter betrayal?

It was Mauricio, Carlos' father. He had betrayed his son and all the people who had built the business.

Shakespeare couldn't have written a more tortured plot.

You're probably wondering—how could a father be so diabolical? How could he be so cruel to his family members, who relied on his leadership? But, if you consider the very real possibility that Mauricio saw the business as an extension of himself, you realize how much the company meant to him. It was his mistress, his source of social and financial power. But most importantly, it was his identity in the world.

To admit to his son that the business was faltering would be tantamount to admitting his failure as a father and a man. That's heavy psychological terrain to have to traverse.

Mauricio had kept failure at bay by hiding the problems and keeping Carlos completely out of the loop.

Here's how Carlos put it: "I could have prevented it if I'd had a bit of forewarning. I would have put together a group of investors and made the same or slightly better offer to my father. It is very hard to anticipate the signs of betrayal by a father because we have a relationship and loyalty to the person who betrays us, and as a result, we fully trust that person. And that prevents us from admitting the possibility of negative events. This is even more true in a family business."

Carlos could not conceive of his father betraying him and his family to prop up his own ego, and therefore he missed any possible red flags. He believed that keeping the legacy alive was all that his father needed. He could not anticipate the sting of failure that his father was keeping at bay, and how the sale could bolster his flagging ego.

This is a frequent occurrence in family businesses. Family members cannot conceive that their own family can undermine them, but it happens. And a parent betraying his or her own child is the worst type of betrayal. Mauricio's unpredictability and unwillingness to show any sign of weakness to his son leveled a company and ruined his employees' lives.

Do you think a sister's betrayal might be better or worse than a father's betrayal? Read Mimi's story to understand how the level of destruction can be equally catastrophic.

SISTERS: CAN'T LIVE WITH THEM, CAN'T LIVE WITHOUT THEM

Mimi picked up the phone to call her jeweler. A few weeks ago, she'd gotten her mother's three-band diamond ring divided into single bands, one for each of her daughters. Now that her mother was in the throes of serious dementia, Mimi wanted to ensure that her daughters had a happy and lasting remembrance of their grandmother, one that in time, they would give to their own daughters.

"Jess, sorry it's taken me so long to pick up my rings, but I'll be there tomorrow. The business has me 24/7."

"It's okay, Mimi; your sister Mandy picked them up last week," the jeweler replied cheerfully.

Mimi said goodbye to Jess and slammed down her phone. Mandy had pulled another fast one.

Even though the three sisters—Mimi, Mandy, and Meg—had agreed that each would choose one piece of jewelry from their mother's collection, Mandy clearly wasn't satisfied. As always, she wanted more.

Meg, as usual, was in the office with Mimi. At their father's request, and supported by his leadership, the two had co-led the family handbag business that their dad had started, and with creativity and hard work, they had built upon his initial success. After their father's stroke, they took the reins of the business and never let go. They were proud of the growth they had created and were at the point of discussing the possibility of a sale in order to continue to build the brand through a global parent company.

"Meg, our dear sister has just pulled off a jewel heist," Mimi said, followed by an explanation of what had just happened.

"Call her on it," Meg said angrily.

It was not a great conversation, but Mimi managed to retrieve the rings from Mandy's grasp.

Mandy had very different priorities than her sisters. She never wanted anything to do with the business, except, of course, for endorsing the checks for her share of the profits. It was maddening, but typical of Mandy's sense of entitlement. It had not helped that their father—despite the fact that Mimi and Meg were running the business—had insisted *that since there were three sisters, the profits were always to be split three ways. And he memorialized this requirement in his will.*

Mandy and her husband, Dave, were a never-ending source of drag and drama on the sisters and the business. Dave fed Mandy conspiracy theories about how Meg and Mimi were taking advantage of her by running the business and keeping all the money for themselves. He further agitated Mandy by telling her that her two sisters were paying themselves oversized salaries and bonuses, which diminished the amount of profit that all three shared.

In fact, he thought he could watch out for Mandy's interests by proclaiming himself CEO. Even though he had no experience in retailing, distribution, or resourcing, Dave thought that being a man who was married to Mandy was reason enough to take over everything. As he constantly told them all, "If your father had a son, he would be running the business, not you girls. Well, by marrying Mandy, I am his son, so I have the right to run the business."

Mimi and Meg never gave in to his demand, and, fortunately, he had no legal right to make it happen. But now that they were ready to sell the business, they weren't sure what obstacles Mandy and Dave would throw in their path.

The terms of their father's trust dictated that all three sisters had to agree to the terms of a sale. As Mimi and Meg closed in on a deal, they wondered how Mandy would react to the news.

"She is so greedy that she'll grab the cash and leave us alone," Meg offered. "Even though she makes us crazy, I'm sure she will do what's best for all of us. Don't forget, we are still all sisters."

A month later, they had made a firm deal for the sale and were elated by the terms. Even Mandy and Dave were impressed. So it was with a sigh of relief that the three sisters raised a glass of champagne to celebrate the final deal and the next day's signing.

"I'm so excited!" Mandy gushed. "It's a dream come true after all our work!"

Mimi and Meg quietly responded with raised eyebrows. In the vestibule of their lawyer's office the next day, Mandy made an announcement.

"One small detail. I want you both to know that I deserve a one million dollar bonus," Mandy said.

Mimi was furious. Meg couldn't believe her ears.

"You what? You want a bonus? For making us do all the work all these years? Why on Earth would we give you a bonus?" Mimi seethed, deadly calm, though unable to hide her disgust.

"Why, for signing, of course. You know, it's called a 'signing bonus.' You're the business people; I'm sure you have heard that term before. If you don't give it to me, I don't sign. It's really simple," Mandy declared with a sickening smile.

Whoever said that blood is thicker than water was wrong. Mandy's betrayal of a family bond showed how little family can matter when greed is involved.

Meg and Mimi had no choice. Mandy received her money and the deal was closed. As was their sisterly relationship. Forevermore.

Mimi's story is a perfect example of how families can work for the good of the business or against it. Despite the ease and success Mimi had with Meg, the ownership agreement required that all three sisters had to agree on financial terms in order to sell the company. It was a powder keg, ripe for betrayal when least expected.

As Harry Levinson explains, "The fundamental psychological conflict in family businesses is rivalry, compounded by feelings of guilt, when more than one family member is involved."[18]

Mimi learned the hard way that you never know which family

---

18 Levinson, "Conflicts That Plague Family Businesses."

member will stab you in the back and when it will happen. Of course, Mandy's greed and sense of entitlement, coupled with her husband's goading, were significant red flags. Mimi and Meg were constantly on edge, awaiting Mandy's unreasonable demands. But they were not prepared for Mandy's last-minute money grab and potential hijacking of the company sale.

The next epic family saga recalls Marcy Syms's earlier warning that businesses that function like families cannot survive. Cynthia and Dick's story demonstrates what happens when family and business roles and goals collide.

DO YOU TAKE THIS WOMAN TO LOVE, HONOR, AND BETRAY?

Cynthia was vaguely aware of the difficulty that working with one's husband could cause, but she pushed it into a back corner of her mind. She and her husband, Dick, had co-founded a company that was growing slowly. It was quite a feat, given that they had four young children.

At first, Cynthia followed the unspoken rules of her conservative background, and stayed at home to care for their children while Dick took on the critical role of CEO. But once the children were in school, she had time to help with their growing business. There was no end to the work that had to be done, and few employees to do it, so Cynthia took on back-office responsibilities, including finance and proposal writing, while Dick continued to lead the company.

It worked well, until Cynthia's responsibilities continued to increase and she found herself becoming a major influence on the direction and future of the company. She loved the fact that she was consulted on all major decisions and that Dick championed her ideas for new growth opportunities. Soon, however, Dick started to talk about his increasing stress level and desire for some time away from the business. He surprised Cynthia with a novel suggestion.

"Hey, love, time for an honest conversation. You're the one doing all the strategizing and hiring," he began. "You like it, and you're really good at it. Why not take over as CEO? Truth is, after all the time I've put in as the face of the company, I'm ready to step back and breathe. I can be a great stay-at-home dad."

Flattered and excited, Cynthia thought it through and came back to Dick with a few conditions.

"Since the original structure of the company reflected your role as CEO, I think it's fair that we redo the structure and make me a 50 percent owner, and I will take the CEO's salary," she told him. "Also, we need to be clear about defining your new role—if you even want one."

Dick pushed back at first, but finally, he agreed to Cynthia's terms, even though he had to reduce his salary—and given his decreased involvement in the business, he agreed that doing so made sense.

Initially, Dick was thrilled. To maximize his flexibility, he took on a part-time consulting role with their company and arranged his days around the children's schedules: school, sports, and other activities. This easy transition, however, did not last very long.

Soon, Dick was unhappy. While he enjoyed more flexibility and less stress, he missed the power and recognition of his former CEO role. Running the household was tedious and there was no reward, no praise for a job well done. He hated being home, but instead of admitting it, he began to disparage Cynthia's skills and he constantly sabotaged her in front of their children. But Cynthia chose to brush his behavior aside. She believed it was simply Dick trying to bolster his self-esteem after forgoing his CEO status. When she addressed his behavior, he denied it and refused to discuss how they might regain their former close relationship.

Cynthia continued to drive the growth of the company. She hired new employees. Her executive team developed new products and services. She formed a board and became chairman as well as CEO. As a consultant, Dick should not have been on the board, but as a 50 percent owner, he was a voting member.

That's when more trouble began. Dick's anger at his self-imposed marginalization and his refusal to acknowledge his feelings played out in front of the employees. He began finding reasons to come in to the office and criticize the company's success and direction. He also undermined Cynthia's proposals to the board.

"You know, Cynthia, you'll just devalue the business if you make this boneheaded move," he would say whenever a new product was discussed.

He became so intrusive and obnoxious, employees threatened to quit.

At home, Dick's assaults intensified. He read Cynthia's emails and continued the criticism in front of the children. He would read something aloud and ask them to find the flaws in it, rewarding them when they were able to do so. He became constantly vicious and vengeful, and Cynthia felt betrayed. She had trusted the strength of their relationship and his desire to step down from the CEO position. She had done nothing other than make good on his offer, and now she was being punished for it.

Cynthia tried everything to calm him down and help him salvage his ego, but nothing helped.

Despite his denials about his behavior, Cynthia insisted on counseling and he finally agreed. Here, he poured out his anger and resentment. He was angry that she was running the business. In truth, he couldn't accept the fact that she was a far more effective and successful CEO than he had been, and worse, she loved the job. Just as it appeared that there was hope for their relationship, he suddenly refused to continue with counseling, and his behavior continued as before.

In desperation, Cynthia sought out a divorce lawyer, who confirmed what she suspected and feared.

"You're working eighteen-hour days and he's home most of the time, so that will affect the divorce judgment," he told her. "He may well win full custody."

Cynthia decided to take her chances, and announced her intentions to divorce Dick.

"Dick, we have a family and a business to run," she declared. "Your attitude and behavior is destroying everything we have built. I can't watch the destruction any longer. I'm taking our four kids and moving out. It's over."

The shock that registered in Dick's face was electrifying. It appeared that he was finally seeing the impact of his bad behavior.

Tearfully, he suggested a return to counseling, promising to do all that it took to save their family. Cynthia eventually agreed to try once again. By working to understand the events that so traumatized him, he saw that he had thought his wife had betrayed him. From his point of view, Cynthia had stolen his identity and left his ego battered. He'd felt he was acting out of self-defense to keep his self-esteem despite her betrayal.

They left each of these sessions agreeing to do better. They wanted to reconnect and revive a deep relationship without jealousy or recrimination. In the end, the couple determined that love trumped anger.

Today, Dick works at another company while Cynthia continues as chairman and CEO of the company they cofounded. Both have rearranged their schedules to spend more time as a family unit. Simple things, like enjoying dinners together, are helping to put them on the path to a better future.

Dick and Cynthia felt each had betrayed the other. Despite this, they thought they could compartmentalize their anger about their work roles and not have it bleed into their roles as parents and spouses. It did not work, nor was there any possibility that this could be a viable solution to their sense of mutual betrayal. As this excerpt by Benjamin Means in the *William & Mary Law Review* on the challenges of family business notes, "Such a position seems very unrealistic in that it expects family members to behave like strangers toward each other. Family members do not expect to deal with one another at arm's length, let alone like the rational actors posited by economic theory."[19]

In other words, emotions intersect the roles of parent, spouse, and business partner. These emotions can spark feelings of betrayal and a desire for retribution. In the case of Cynthia and Dick, they traveled that unhappy path for a long time, but, with reflection and intervention, moved on to openness, remorse, and finally, reconciliation.

As you will see next in Carolyn's story, feeling marginalized and seeking revenge can also happen when the line between family and "like family" is blurred.

HE'S JUST LIKE FAMILY

Carolyn's father, Pete, collected businesses and properties the way some people collect vintage cars. And when he discovered the rural beauty of the Upper Peninsula of Michigan, he packed up the family and spent most summers there.

It was a beautiful location, full of forests and rolling hills. Carolyn marveled at her dad's instinct for great real estate. He purchased houses, rented them out, and, always wanting more, even signed for three thousand acres of raw land. His businesses were a varied lot, from the village apparel store to a towing operation—very different from his businesses in the city.

Pete became friendly with a local couple, Don and Susie Marshall, who agreed to look after the properties while Pete, his wife, and family

---

19 Means, *William & Mary Law Review.*

were away. The two families became close over the years, celebrating holidays and special events together. And with every passing year, Don and Susie felt and were treated more and more like family.

Pete was kind enough to build them a house—at no cost—close to the one in which Pete's family lived.

Sadly, Pete died unexpectedly of a heart attack, and his death created many issues. The family agreed they couldn't continue to manage the portfolio of businesses and properties that Pete had so deftly built. So they all agreed it was best to sell off the properties, land, and businesses. The family asked Carolyn, the oldest daughter and a skilled business executive, to lead the divestiture.

Carolyn took this responsibility very seriously, and her first step was to gain a clear picture of what Don had been managing.

"Be glad to be of help, darlin'," Don said and smiled condescendingly. "But it'll take a little time. Your daddy had me doing lots of things for him. I'll try to write it all down."

Time passed, and Carolyn was becoming impatient, so she went next door to once again find Don. Susie opened up the screen door and uncharacteristically kept Carolyn on the porch.

"Hi, Susie. I need to see Don; it's important," Carolyn said gently.

"Gosh … I'll ah … tell him, soon as he comes home," Susie stammered nervously.

When Carolyn was finally able to force Don to meet, it seemed every time she asked a question, he had an excuse as to why he didn't have the answer. For a long while, Carolyn chalked it up to a slower-paced, small-town world and Don's lack of experience in business.

But that all changed when she met Neil, a professional forester, at a conference in Minnesota.

She hired Neil to take a look at the raw land and give his professional opinion on how to best prepare for a sale. His first report was a startling one. *A large number of acres had been cut down for timber.*

"*That's impossible; my dad would never do such a thing,*" *she told Neil. "There is no record of that anywhere."*

But this was just the start. Immediately, Carolyn began looking closer and digging deeper. Don, the trusted family friend, caretaker, and neighbor had cut and sold the timber. She then discovered far more assaults on the family. Don had allowed people to hunt on the properties for a fee. And he and Susie rented out the family house whenever the family wasn't there—yet another in the growing list of true betrayals of the family's trust.

This was all done for Don's personal gain. The betrayals stung deeply, because Don and his wife had woven themselves into the fabric of Carolyn's family. Thankfully, Carolyn caught up with the extensive deceptions and was able to out the culprit and staunch the damage. Don, in an attempt to defend himself, told Carolyn all he was doing was ensuring that he had a "pension" plan for whenever Carolyn's family decided to sell the proper-ties. He defended his actions by saying he had spent his life taking care of them with nothing to help him once he retired or they left, whichever came first. Amazingly, he refused to see these actions as betrayals, or even as theft of property. He saw them as fully justifiable.

Although Carolyn threatened to sue Don and force him to repay all he had stolen, the family decided that it was not worth the effort and that there would be much to lose with little to gain. Carolyn hadn't been aware of Don's fear of the future that had led him to cheat and steal. In hindsight, Carolyn recognized she should have been more open about the family's plans for her father's assets. She could have tempered Don's desperation by giving him time to rethink his future and possibly providing some financial cushion.

Carolyn also realized she'd trusted Don and Susie blindly, and had considered them family, even though they were not. She'd assumed they would act as family and threw suspicion to the wind. Even when Don deliberately avoided her, she didn't use wise trust to determine whether or not what he had been telling her was truthful. She had pictured Don as harmless, someone who only had the best interests of her family at heart.

Since Pete, Carolyn's father, had not set clear boundaries, roles, or oversight expectations at the outset, Don assumed an independent role in the business with no oversight, lines of responsibility, or accountability. Indeed, he felt entitled to all that he took. It's a common trap and a perfect setup for betrayal. Because Don felt like a member of the family, he acted with that authority.

Most family businesses have unspoken or rarely defined norms and expectations regarding behavior toward family members. The reason? Core family values serve as a basis for acceptable and unacceptable behaviors as it relates to the operation of business. So, it's no surprise an outsider isn't beholden to those values or expected to live by them, and it's why, in these situations, betrayal may well be on the horizon.

Our final story of this chapter pits the family against an aggressive and manipulative opportunist.

NEVER UNDERESTIMATE EGO

Tara's dad, Roger, was an eighty-year-old tiger. His business acumen and incredible drive pushed each of his ventures into the stratosphere.

Naturally, he involved his family in any big decisions, as they were all part of his "collective enterprise."

Two years earlier, Tara convinced her dad that it was time to put the brakes on his business involvements and begin enjoying life with his friends, children, and grandchildren.

Reluctantly, he agreed. He was happy to reconnect with old buddies and interests, but as the months went by, the itch to sniff out opportunity and create yet another success returned. Quite simply, he realized that his favorite hobby was building successful businesses.

Enter Jim, Roger's former chief of staff, who invited him out for lunch.

"Business or pleasure, Jim?" Roger asked.

"You be the judge," Jim answered.

Lunch turned into Jim's passionate presentation of how a specific market need was just waiting to be exploited, and his perfect idea as to how to do so.

"Roger, you're the only person with the experience to pull this off. Risky, yes, but hey, we've been there before. Just think about it," Jim said with a tempting gleam in his eye.

It didn't take Roger long to jump right in.

Tara understood her father's need to return to the world that he loved and leave retirement behind. And so she watched as her dad began researching, organizing, and strategizing the new business. Unsurprisingly, Jim was given a significant equity stake and the title of president. And Roger asked Tara to become the interim CFO.

The initial excitement and early success of the venture fueled Roger's ego. He still had it. And with Jim at his side, nothing could stop him. He was delighted by the idea that this new business would become a growing family business with lots of opportunity for his grandchildren. Not only that, but it would burnish his legacy.

While the kids were happy their father was so engaged, they worried about Jim's constant requests for more money, more staff, and more plane tickets. Tara was in charge of signing off on expenses, and, as she told her siblings, they seemed exorbitant for a start-up.

Tara cautioned her father about these out-of-control expenses, but he

ignored her. She went to her siblings for support, and, while they under-
stood and were concerned about her observations, they told her to tread
lightly so as not to upset their father. It seemed Jim had convinced Roger
that he alone was the business builder, and he alone would determine
the allocation of funds. Soon, Roger listened to no one's advice but Jim's.

"For God's sake, forget Tara's interference," Jim told Roger. "She's no
visionary. That's your department. She's worried about finances because
she wants to protect the family's inheritance. These petty concerns about
expenses are short-sighted because we're about to double that inheritance."

Meanwhile, Jim milked the assets and skimmed some for himself. Yet
Roger's faith never wavered, even when disturbing facts began to surface.
The family discovered Jim had lied about focus group results, market
potential, and production costs. The house of cards was crumbling.

For Roger, it was the ultimate shame to learn how badly he had been
taken, and how he was now jeopardizing everything he'd built for his heirs.

Overwhelmed by embarrassment, Roger began to wind down the
business. He was extremely stressed and depressed. He could not admit
that he had been betrayed by Jim and had bought the deception to feed
his aging ego. It was too much, and sadly, soon after, Roger died.

Here, too, is a case of blind trust run amuck.

It took Tara and the family years to untangle Jim's financial
manipulations. To do so and salvage the losses, they realized that
they would need to make the business a top priority.

To this day, everyone blames Jim for his betrayal. Jim effectively
cut Roger off from his family by painting them as naysayers. Jim
stoked conflict by convincing him the family was sabotaging his
last great business achievement. But in the end, it was Roger who
betrayed his family by refusing to listen to their issues. Roger's blind
trust in Jim overpowered his family's attempts to help him find a way

to wise trust. Although they constantly alerted him to Jim's deceit, he chose his own ego over family wisdom.

Tara is still living with the consequences of that conflict as she faces the challenge of salvaging her father's business and preventing further losses.

When a family is involved in a business, negotiations are anything but typical because expectations are unspoken and hurt feelings cut even deeper.

"It's not personal; it's just business" does not apply. Even a simple misunderstanding can be seen as betrayal. Unlike in other business relationships, this involves a vortex of emotions, which can include past rivalries, broken promises, and underlying drama.

Betrayal in a family business can be so damaging because it flatlines trust. There is no calm compromise or meeting of the minds because it's *all* personal. And that's what makes a family business so difficult to successfully manage. When you consider that a family unit is based on shared bonds and values, it's easy to see how much can go wrong if even just one person goes rogue.

As George Stalk and Henry Foley, family business advisors, observe, "It's unrealistic to think you can create a nepotism-free family-owned business, and it's important to recognize that family enterprises will always operate by different rules. To survive over the long haul, family firms need to adopt formal policies about whom to employ, whom to promote, and how to balance family and business interests. If more companies take these steps and survive the treacherous transitions from one generation to another, everyone will benefit."[20]

---

20 Stalk, "Avoid the Traps That Can Destroy Family Businesses."

TAKEAWAYS

1. Blind trust has no place in a family business. Wise trust applies to family and non-family businesses equally.

2. Never assume employees who are treated like family will act like family. Their loyalties and allegiances are to their family members, not yours.

3. Family members are never "at will" employees.

4. Business partners who are marital partners make very difficult bedfellows.

5. Audit reports by outside non-family members are a smart source of oversight.

6. Ego can trump rationality and loyalty to family.

7. Board members who are friends think as friends, not as independent advisors.

8. Family businesses have both business goals and family goals, never confuse the two.

9. Set policies and guidelines because casual, ad hoc operations are easy pickings for betrayers.

10. Just because an outside manager is a shareholder doesn't guarantee his or her honesty.

11. Think long and hard about setting up a family business. Do not do so if you cannot run it as a meritocracy with the proper controls, structure, and processes in place.

CHAPTER FIVE

Yes, Revenge Is Sweet, but Karma Is Sweeter

Life is an echo. What you send out comes back.
—Zig Ziglar

Many of us nurture a fantasy of revenge after even the smallest slight. It fuels our dreams of the perfect putdown and the ultimate win, pulling the curtain back on the betrayer's true character. Yet most of us choose to move forward, never turning the fantasy into reality.

Revenge is a special type of punishment. It involves an act of reciprocal morality also known as "payback." If the betrayer refuses to own the trauma and pain of the betrayed, then the desire for revenge increases. Forgiveness is virtually impossible if the betrayer will not take responsibility for his or her deeds. If that's the case, revenge may become an attractive option. But as you will see in this chapter, taking revenge on your betrayer can prevent you from moving on with your life. Then again, some of our survivors have found that it can, in special circumstances, help them move forward.

So if active revenge isn't the answer, many people look to karma and the mysterious workings of the universe. Karma is a Hindu and Buddhist belief that an individual's actions can determine their future. It means that if someone misbehaves, they will ultimately—in this life or the next—be punished for their betrayal. There is no time limit on karma, and while it doesn't usually carry the zing of instant gratification, it can be even more soul satisfying.

When the betrayer shows no remorse for the betrayal, the betrayed can choose to:

- seek and take revenge,

- let the anger fester and build,

- repress or deny the betrayal,

- forgive the betrayer, or

- move on without granting forgiveness.

Each reaction has a unique impact on one's ability to move forward and build a new future. As a result of our research and interviews, we have learned that regaining power is only possible through options four and five. As you will see in the next chapter, there are many types of forgiveness. Even when no form of forgiveness is acceptable to the person betrayed, it is still possible to move forward.

In the following stories, only one of the four people who suffered betrayal opted for revenge. Ambushed by betrayers, and hurt by breaches of trust, our survivors were infuriated by the circumstances that defined their new reality. Of course, they wished for a humiliating takedown of their betrayer, but, despite this wish, most did not choose to engage in revenge for its own sake. They made considered decisions (here's the notion of strategic patience again) to manage their betrayal and remain true to their own values and moral compass.

Let's begin with Austin, who was betrayed by the managing partner of the law firm where she had worked since her graduation from law school. As you read this, it's important to realize Austin's story took place years ago, when such discussions were not illegal, and sadly were commonplace.

PROMISES MADE, PROMISES UNKEPT

A high-powered law firm recruited Austin based on her excellent academic credentials and intense work ethic. Her reputation for court wins put her in an enviable position. She was clearly on a direct path to becoming a partner.

After yet another success, she squared her shoulders and marched into the office of Mac, the managing partner, to deliver the big ask.

"Mac, it's time for an honest and direct conversation," she began.

"I suspect I'm about to hear yet another recital of your sterling record in the courtroom that ends in a request for partnership," he said, staring at the ceiling. "That would make you not only the first female partner, but the first mama-to-be partner."

"My pregnancy has nothing to do with my work," Austin stated firmly.

"Really? Then let's see what you can do with this," Mac replied as he tossed a case file at Austin. "Win it, and I agree: you'll get your prize."

She scooped up the scattered documents and walked out the door.

Austin began to review what this case would entail. It didn't take long to realize her assignment was a setup, but a setup that held opportunity.

And that's how Austin pushed aside her anger to work on Mac's impossible case with a positive attitude.

She convened her team of associates, dug into research, took each deposition herself, and carefully reviewed each and every fact. It was an arduous process that claimed her days and nights. Thankful for a husband that encouraged her ambition and workaholism, Austin kept her focus.

To everyone's surprise, Austin won the case. It was a victory she savored and the partners appreciated.

Every partner, that is, except Mac, the boss who controlled her future.

"Awfully lucky," he managed to spit out at her celebratory lunch.

The next day, Austin asked Mac's assistant, Jesse, if Mac was in.

"Sure, he's all yours," Jesse replied as she swung open the door to Mac's office.

Austin sensed this would be a defining moment, and she was completely prepared.

"Yes?" he asked, not looking up from his reading.

"I lived up to my end of the deal. Now it's your turn."

The silence hung heavy and long in every corner of the room.

"It always comes to this, doesn't it, my dear?" he finally said. "Sorry, but you'll have to choose motherhood or the legal profession. No room for both. We can't have an absent partner while you're off being a mama, can we?"

"But I understood—," Austin replied.

"Apparently, not well enough," Mac retorted. "We don't have female partners, especially those with children."

It was a startling conversation—one that Jesse had overheard. As Austin left Mac's office, Jesse followed her and handed her an envelope. Jesse had written up what she'd overheard from all of Austin's conversations with Mac, and—amazingly—had also added a previously compiled and notarized list of complaints from other women who had been treated similarly by Mac.

"As you can see, you're not the first one of his female 'rejects,'" Jesse explained.

Austin's first response was to find a way to revenge his betrayal. As she considered her options, she realized that even though Mac had taken the low road, she wanted to take the high road and move on. So she walked out the door. Out of the firm. And out from under Mac's archaic notion about women practicing law.

Eighteen months later, having just made partner at a bigger firm, Austin took a phone call from the White House Counsel's Office. They wanted references for Mac, who was up for a federal judgeship. Austin described her experience with the prospective appointee in detail. She even offered up proof by way of the notarized write-up Jesse had given her. But it wasn't necessary, because other women in Mac's past employ had told the same story. Needless to say, Mac never became a federal judge.

For Austin, taking the high road and leaving with her dignity intact was a perfect defense against the betrayal. When asked, she admits she wished for revenge, but she notes that she did not want to compromise her integrity by seeking it at the time. She also admits that she had many fantasies about the types of revenge that she could take, but none were as powerful a revenge as that call about the judgeship. Wanting revenge is all about evening the score. In Austin's case, that phone call was a perfect example of distributive justice. Her "reference" for Mac couldn't prevent further bad behavior on his part, but it did right a wrong for Austin and all the other smart, talented women he had betrayed. By waiting and then punishing a violation, Austin showed the value of strategic patience and reaffirmed her sense of honor and personal sense of self.

Many factors determine your response to betrayal. Emotional makeup is key, as is your history of dealing with stress and other negative situations. Your culture, values, and beliefs also play a strong role in deciding if revenge is the right road to take. The sting of public embarrassment and damage to your reputation can often result in wanting to take active revenge. It's the desire to kill or maim, or at least humiliate, the beast and ruin the betrayer. The desire for revenge is very different than the desire for punishment. Peg Streep, a prolific author on this and similar topics, notes that revenge seeks to have the betrayer suffer while a punisher seeks to improve the betrayer's behavior or to deter future bad behavior.[21]

In Austin's story, her initial wish to seek revenge was not due to low self-esteem, but rather, her high self-esteem was challenged by the act of betrayal. Mac's denial of her partnership reaffirmed her lack of power and made a mockery of her competence through no fault of her own. Often, revenge is seen as the only way to save face and rebalance the power lost through betrayal.

Does exacting revenge work? Michael Price, staff editor of the American Psychological Association's *Monitor on Society*, reviews several studies on the outcomes of revenge, and observes that it can backfire by compromising one's integrity and reaching down to the nasty level of the betrayer.[22] It's even worse, according to Professor Kevin Carlsmith, based on his testing of responses to revenge: "Rather than providing closure, it does the opposite: it keeps the wound open and fresh."[23]

The question then, is how to successfully balance your need for revenge with your need to maintain your personal integrity and stature. Because the danger is that sometimes, the one seeking

---

21   Streep, "The Psychology of Revenge (and Vengeful People)."
22   Price, *Monitor on Society.*
23   Carlsmith, "The Paradoxical Consequences of Revenge."

revenge looks far worse than the betrayer. As many have pointed out, you do not want to give your betrayer something that justifies why you were betrayed. Don't give him or her the opportunity to blame you for any situation that can hurt you in the end.

As one of our survivors noted, "I cannot spend my life in bitterness. I need to focus on all the opportunities and successes I've had. If I take revenge, I'm just as bad."

Another survivor said, "I think of revenge all the time. I wish my betrayer all of the worst, but it's not up to me; it's up to a higher power. I'm really not a vengeful person."

The next three stories of Amy, Kathleen, and Allen are more examples of karmic revenge taking care of the betrayer.

Let's begin with Amy.

KICKED OFF THE TEAM, BUT STILL KICKING

She was known as "Amy Acquisition," even in her role as a freelance consultant for a consumer goods company. So when the CEO, Eli, decided to acquire a fast-growing business, he came to Amy with an offer to join him full time and become part of the acquisition team.

"Eli, you know me. I love to consult because, if necessary, I can tell clients that the emperor has no clothes. Unlike an employee, I do not need to be politically correct or polite. I am hired to tell the truth, no matter how difficult."

"Amy, that's what I want. Your honesty and ability to highlight issues with the board and me is key," he said reassuringly. "I promise, as long as you bring your critical thinking to the table, I'll be a happy man."

Amy came on board as chief administrative officer and EVP, as well as secretary to the board, as Eli had little confidence in the current secretary.

She was welcomed by the executive heading the acquisition, Randy, a suave character who was being groomed by Eli as the next CEO.

As the acquisition proceeded, Amy dealt with many bumps in the road. What made these bumps unique was that they were not caused by the company they were hoping to acquire. Instead, these obstacles were the result of Eli's and Randy's disdain for the CEO on the other side of the table.

Amy watched as promises were made publicly to the other CEO, but rescinded in private by Randy. This rattled Amy and she went to Eli with her concerns about the integrity of the process.

"Amy, this isn't like you to be such a Girl Scout," Eli said. "But, of course, I'll speak to Randy. I'm sure you're misunderstanding the situation. Don't worry, he'll clear it all up for you."

After the "talk," Randy curbed his behavior for a time, but consistently sidelined Amy, cutting her out of important meetings and rarely asking her opinion.

The CEO of the other company began calling Amy to register his complaints about how he was being treated, and intimated that he was planning on calling off the acquisition, as he could no longer trust Randy and Eli. As the acquisition stumbled, the board called in Amy to ask if Randy was up to the task.

"I think Eli can more fully answer that question," she replied.

When the board pushed for more information, she told them she did not have enough details to respond, as she was no longer included in many of the meetings. She strongly encouraged the board to speak with Eli and Randy.

The day after the meeting, Eli burst in to Amy's office.

"How dare you imply problems with Randy by playing naïve with the board? Why are you trying to kill this acquisition? Your constant meddling is hurting Randy's ability to get this done," he thundered. "I need you to stop thinking and stop talking. You are no longer on the acquisition team."

"So what's my new job description?" she challenged.

"Scrubbing toilets," he countered.

Burning with fury, Amy left the office and went home. That weekend she went shopping and bought the most expensive toilet brush on the planet ... and charged it to her company credit card.

The next day, she placed the brush on the glass conference table where everyone could see it.

As Eli walked by the conference room, he came to a complete stop and yelled, "What the hell is that?"

"Since scrubbing toilets is my new job, I thought it'd be good to have the right tool and a daily reminder. And I think it's time we discussed my severance package," Amy said flatly.

Eli and Amy severed their relationship.

A few months later, after Amy had landed another executive position, she got a call from a law firm.

They needed to depose her regarding some unusual backdating of options during the acquisition deal, a deal hadn't gone through. Amy asked for a copy of the compensation committee minutes that they were describing. All were signed "notwithstanding" before her name.

"Yes, that is my signature, but I never was a witness to those grants, and I've never used the term 'notwithstanding,'" Amy explained. "It's a legal term and I'm not a lawyer. Check out all my earlier compensation committee minutes to see how I have always signed the minutes."

Eli was removed as CEO for SEC violations.

The general counsel was disbarred for forging minutes and aiding in the backdating of options.

Randy was fired for destroying the possibility of the acquisition for all the reasons Amy had previously raised.

When asked why she had gone quietly, rather than going to the board, Amy explained that she'd decided not to behave as badly as Eli and Randy. And if the board had wanted to know the whole truth, they would have come to her.

They never did.

For Amy, now sitting in the executive suite of her new company, the new, sweet taste of karmic revenge and vindication more than made up for the bitter taste of betrayal.

There are times when karmic revenge happens in a nanosecond, and others when more patience and faith in the universe are required. We will see the payoff of patience and faith in Casey's story:

SURVIVAL TRUMPS REVENGE

Casey heard the knock on her hotel room door at 2:00 a.m. She knew at once it was her boss, Don, known by all as "The Lech."

"Hey, sweetie, it's me—you know—the guy in charge of your high-flying career," he crooned in a drunken drawl.

Casey turned over in her bed, hoping Angie—her fashion-coordinator roommate—was asleep in her bed. Of course she wasn't, because this was the City of Lights, and Angie's first buying trip. The knocking continued until Casey's will to ignore Don shut him down.

Casey wasn't surprised by Don's crudeness. The whisper network revealed that every female at the company had a tale about this fat, arrogant boor. As protection, women always traveled in pairs to international business meetings and dinners when Don would be present.

But what surprised Casey was Don's changed behavior after Paris. He treated her respectfully after that middle-of-the-night incident. In fact, in the months that followed, Casey began to develop a workable relationship with Don, who suddenly wanted to become her mentor, no strings attached.

She remained cautiously optimistic as Don recommended a promotion for her, which made her the youngest vice president in the company's history. She began to think that perhaps she had been overly tough on him and needed to be less cynical and suspicious.

And then it was the Christmas rush. Two nights before the big holiday, Casey was helping out at the flagship store and thought she was alone in the stockroom rechecking an inventory report, when suddenly she felt a deliberate hand travel under her skirt. She turned around and saw Don leering at her. Casey's reaction was strong and swift. She pushed Don into the shelves and they crashed down around him.

His face erupted in total rage.

Caught by surprise and somewhat confused, Casey apologized to Don as he collected himself from the floor.

"Clean up this mess, and if you ever say a word to anyone, your career is over," he declared dramatically.

Don had gone from predator to benefactor and back to predator. Casey's trust had been betrayed.

Shaken and unnerved, she told her female boss what had happened.

"Grow up. Welcome to the world. Just deal with it," the woman advised. "Or forget about going anywhere in this business."

This can't be right, Casey thought to herself. So she made the decision go to human resources, and lodged a complaint. Here, too, she was betrayed.

The VP was sympathetic, but firm in his counsel.

"He is a senior executive and you are not. He is also responsible for mentoring and promoting you. You should be grateful, not vindictive. You are talking career suicide."

When Casey protested, it was agreed by all it would be better if she found another job. This, despite the fact that she had just been promoted.

And the final betrayal? Casey's fiancé blamed the trouble on her flirtatious behavior.

"Maybe you send mixed messages. It's not his fault if he misinterprets your behavior. Anyway, Casey, going to HR was a dumb move. You should be smarter than that," he added, making it even worse.

Casey had two decisions to make. If she continued to address the betrayal of her trust, she'd lose her job and her hopes of succeeding in the industry. She was worried that any form of revenge would result in further harm to her career. So she moved forward and found another position in another part of the country. She succeeded in building a strong career, despite periodically hearing that Don was still saying negative things about her.

She also dumped her fiancé.

Casey was content that her revenge took the form of moving on and building a spectacular career without sacrificing her morals. But the universe added a dash of delicious payback.

Many years later, Casey was at an industry benefit. By chance, she was placed at a table where Don and his wife, along with others from her business past, were seated. Bizarrely, Don was the only man at the table. How weirdly appropriate, *Casey thought.* This should be interesting.

Dinner was served. Polite conversation ensued until Don's wife posed a question.

"Is there anyone here who has not *been sexually harassed by my husband?" She asked.*

Not one of the seven other women at the table raised her hand. Don's wife threw her wine in his face. She laughed bitterly, and walked out of the room, followed closely by a groveling Don. The women at the table gave one another knowing smiles and celebrated with a toast. Karma may have taken its sweet time, but the wait was worthwhile.

In the days before the power of #MeToo, Casey's decision to move on was easy. She realized that if she focused on revenge, her career would be destroyed, and given HR's response, no one would believe her. She also knew that her only way to survive was to get out of the company's toxic environment. She wanted to stay in the industry and build her career. In some ways, the betrayals she experienced created a personal survival guide. As we discussed in Chapter Two, Casey developed her own cheater-detector mechanisms, which helped her through many a tough situation. She became a master of employing wise trust and reading red flags.

The dinner with Don and his wife was karma on steroids. Seeing the joy on Casey's face as she describes that event is memorable, and proof that if you hang in there long enough, you just may see bad deeds come back to hurt, if not haunt, your betrayer.

The next story gives karma another chance to turn the tables on a bad actor.

BULLIES, BAD ACTORS, AND SELF-RESPECT

From the first day Mike walked into Allen's office, Allen knew the guy was power-mad. As the new kid on the block, Mike was ready to grab budgets, people, and credit for anything that had a whiff of ready-made success.

When Mike made the "honest mistake" of giving Allen the wrong start time for a meeting, Allen's instincts were confirmed. It was petty, but it made Allen look careless in front of their boss, whom they both reported to as directors.

Allen had built a strong and cohesive team that worked hard to build trust inside and outside the operation, up and down the chain of command. It was a solid group known for their success and integrity. And he was proud to be their leader.

The constant drumbeat of Mike's aggressiveness was all-pervasive. In addition to the usual behind-the-back putdowns, he questioned Allen's budget expenditures, and even proposed a reorganization that would cause Allen to report to him. It was met with a "We'll take it into consideration" by their boss.

While Allen's team were incensed by Mike's overt attempts to take over, Allen calmed the waters by reminding everyone that good work would speak louder than Mike's obvious attempts at a land-grab.

"Accomplishments are gold," Allen reminded his staff. "And we've got plenty in the bank."

Allen was smart enough to ensure that he stayed on top of Mike's constant sniping and blatant attacks. He was vigilant about countering Mike's "recommendations and observations about how things could be done better," and made sure his boss was aware of each and every goal his group achieved.

But that careful focus was shattered when Allen found out that his younger brother had unexpectedly died, leaving a young family who needed Allen's support. This devastating news sent Allen into deep mourning. He was encouraged to take time off work to help his brother's family, grieve, and recover. Even Mike had the decency to send a sympathetic text. Maybe he wasn't as heartless as Allen had thought.

Two months later, Allen returned to hear that Mike, at the annual meeting, had once again proposed combining his group with Allen's ... while Allen was absent on leave!

"Think of the savings we could realize," Mike had proclaimed. "It would work for everyone. And Allen's personal life has become his priority now and for the future."

Mike's new plan was far more overt, since the earlier, subtler plan had been a failure. He now sought to force Allen's departure via a campaign of bullying and backstabbing. Somehow, he believed that because of Allen's loss, Allen would be more vulnerable and less proactive *in countering the attack.*

Yet again, the people in the room listened but made no decisions. Incredibly, no one tried to defend Allen and put a stop to Mike's constant onslaught.

Allen was dumbfounded that someone would continue to attack him when he was at his most vulnerable. From this point on, Allen chose to avoid Mike. If he ran into him, he was coolly polite, but he made sure his deputy attended Mike's meetings in his place.

As this uncomfortable dance continued, Allen soldiered on. When he spoke with their boss about Mike's constant positioning, he was told that he was being overly sensitive.

"Perhaps you need more time to grieve," his boss suggested. But he did finally admit that Mike's goal was to capture Allen's group for himself. Allen's boss advised him to ignore Mike's actions as he had done in the past, reassuring Allen that the merger of groups would not happen.

Despite support by his colleagues who rallied around him like family, Allen found solace, but no peace. In the end, Allen decided to leave. His brother's death had shown him that life was too short to take constant abuse. He realized Mike's aggressiveness would continue, and their boss would continue to allow it. So nothing would change. Being miserable was no longer an option for Allen. He gave notice and moved on, slowly regaining his confidence and strength.

Two years later, karma came calling. News reached Allen that Mike had finally been given the opportunity to merge the groups, and soon after, he'd been fired for misappropriation of funds. No wonder he had been looking to get his hands on every budget!

In hindsight, Allen realized that Mike's betrayal did not belong to Mike alone. Indeed, as we noted in Chapter One, someone we do not trust cannot betray us, and Allen had never trusted Mike. Mike had been aided and abetted by their boss, who had betrayed Allen's trust through his silence, despite his having watched the scenario play out loud and clear. His silence and refusal to get involved was tacit support of Mike's behavior, so Mike had continued his quest for power at Allen's expense. While Allen had believed that his boss shared his sense of justice and ethical behavior, he later learned that one's behavior is always the best test of one's values. His earlier assumption about his boss had been in error.

He further learned that being vulnerable allows others to step in and push the sword deeper. It has been said that chickens will peck a wounded chicken to death. Just as the coop has a pecking order of social hierarchy, where one chicken is able to peck at and kill another chicken lower in rank, the same can happen in a corporate setting. Allen's betrayal by his boss's constant silence and lack of involvement had signaled to Mike that he could peck at Allen until he surrendered. It appears that karma did not call on everyone who was responsible for Allen's betrayal.

And now we turn to revenge. Of the seventy people we interviewed, Patty, whose story is next up, is the only survivor who decided that revenge was her best way of addressing a betrayal. But then, her betrayal was on two fronts—marriage and business—and, as you will see, she felt that she had nothing left to lose.

A STYLISH REVENGE

Patty owned a successful hair salon on an island, in a resort town just off the California coast. She had worked hard to cultivate the summer crowd as well as her local clientele for all their styling needs.

It was a successful business for a divorcée with two children, and she enjoyed the work.

Sitting at the reception desk one morning, a cheerful gentleman walked through the door, holding a Yorkshire terrier.

"Hello, I'm Rodney," he said with a winning grin. "And I'm a licensed stylist looking for a place to hang my hat."

Patty was very interested, as she needed additional stylists for the summer. Rodney handed her his iPhone and took her through his portfolio.

She was impressed by both Rodney's talent and his manner. It seemed like a smart move to add him to her staff. And, *she thought,* perhaps he can build up our clientele, given his engaging personality.

As they hashed out details of his employment, Rodney had only one request—he wanted his little dog to be with him.

"Not a problem, because he's so well behaved," Patty said, agreeing to his request.

Patty's decision to hire Rodney was a good one. He fit in perfectly with the other stylists and attracted a new crop of clients. And when Patty came down with pneumonia, Rodney stepped in to take over the operation of the salon.

Every day, he stopped by her house go over the day's receipts and show her the appointment book. Rodney charmed both of her children, always taking the time to talk and play with them.

Patty and Rodney became fast, tight friends. Of course, Patty knew he was gay, so she realized a romantic relationship was out of the question. Over the course of the summer and fall, she and her children and Rodney and his dog became something of a family unit.

As the personal side of their relationship grew, so did the professional side. Rodney was now a major part of the business and of her life. He was a partner, friend, father-figure, and even—as unexpected as this was—a romantic interest.

So, it was no surprise to Patty when Rodney proposed to her. She believed him when he told her he was bisexual. Her children were ecstatic, and she welcomed her new future as a married woman, even as she understood that their relationship would be a bit different than that of most heterosexual couples.

They tied the knot, but the marriage crumbled shortly thereafter when Rodney met and fell in love with another man—someone who lived off the island.

"I'm so sorry, Patty," he said as he asked for a divorce. "But this is who I am. Our marriage was a mistake. I got carried away because I care so much for you, but I now realize that it was as a friend, not as a husband."

The marriage was annulled.

This personal disaster also complicated their professional relationship. They could no longer work under one roof. As more of their clients requested that they have their hair styled at home, Patty decided that she enjoyed the flexibility of bringing the salon to the client. So Rodney took over the salon while Patty made house calls to her clients.

This tentative truce lasted until Rodney brought his boyfriend, Aldo, from the mainland to live on the island. He, too, was a stylist, and had a Yorkie just like Rodney's.

Rodney spread the word that Aldo had worked in Paris and Milan, but regardless of his glamorous experience, Aldo's presence unnerved Patty. This was her island and her salon.

But not for long. Soon, Rodney was telling Patty's private clients that Aldo would be happy to style their hair in their home. As Aldo's bookings increased, Patty's fell.

So she planned a wicked revenge. She forged the letterhead from the ASPCA and mailed him a letter detailing a hearing on the mainland where he would be called to address multiple charges of animal abuse. The envelope (also with letterhead) headlined the contents, blaring, "Second Notice to Appear." She also conveniently did not close the envelope, so the enclosed letter was easily accessible by the island postmistress who served as a megaphone for gossip.

The word spread like wildfire. Rodney was vilified, and soon had no clients, despite his protestations of innocence.

Patty took back her salon, and even enjoyed being the subject of a national newspaper article that ran a story on her flourishing business.

As these stories show, revenge can take many forms. Some of the people who were betrayed opted to keep their dignity over revenge, and use their energy to plan a road forward. An appraisal of their own self-worth was key to these decisions. As we noted in Chapter Three, summoning our inner strength at the moment of betrayal can help soften the blow and lessen the damage to our self-esteem.

For Patty, our only *active* revenger, revenge was her route to retaining her self-esteem and power when faced with two people who had taken over her life and livelihood. In Patty's story, she was the victor and her reward was the return of her salon. Clearly, her actions were only possible in light of the culture of the small island where she lived. Her story is a perfect example of distributive justice; she took away Rodney's clients, just as he had done to her. It was a true enactment of "an eye for an eye" justice.

Would this work for you in your situation? Would there be negative repercussions that you did not anticipate? Answering these questions requires time and a strategic perspective.

Understand that the betrayer's goal is to see you humiliated. This person wants you to publicly lose power. The pain that follows is the resultant feelings of inadequacy and shame. So it's important to reclaim your power by finding new ways to disprove the feeling of being unloved and unvalued. The shame belongs to your betrayer. Not to you.

Just as Americans after 9/11 were committed to living their lives without fear to ensure "the terrorists can't win," think of your betrayer as a terrorist. By not letting that person destroy you, you are one step closer to recovery.

It may be hard, but ignore the initial urge to plot and plan a delicious revenge. Planning revenge forces you to continue to live in the betrayal as you spend time and energy trying to find the right and most devious way to revenge it. It continues to provide the betrayer with power over you rather than allowing you to take that power into your own hands. Take the time to wrap yourself in compassion so you can rediscover your core values and sources of personal strength. Through our interviews, survivors tell us it's far more productive to distance yourself from the betrayal and shore up your emotions with rational thoughts. Then, you can clearly derive lessons from the traumatic event and begin planning a better future.

Stress and our reactions to it differ for all of us. So don't worry if your reaction includes anger, ranting, and confrontation, or even the other side of the stress continuum with denial, avoidance, or even short-term withdrawal from the world. The important part is to experience the loss and rage and grieve in your own way as the first step in moving forward.

Remember Austin, who channeled her energy into finding a partnership at another firm? And Amy, who used her anger to shop for a toilet brush? It became the emblem of her betrayal. Casey moved on in a flash when it became clear that she wouldn't stand for sexual harassment or bullying. Allen simply moved forward believing that "living well is the best revenge."

Before you mastermind a well-deserved revenge, remember that many survivors do better and reclaim their power quicker by abstaining from revenge. But then again, think of Patty. Would her solution work for you?

TAKEAWAYS

1. Revenge does not always provide closure; it can do the opposite. It can keep the wound open and fresh, making you weaker and more vulnerable.

2. Revenge can benefit the betrayer more than it benefits you, because it can continue to erode your self-esteem and bolster your sense of being wronged. By doing so, the betrayer retains power over you.

3. Our old friend, strategic patience, is a great tool for giving yourself time to realize you've done nothing wrong—and you *haven't*. So wait a bit before you decide whether or not revenge is the answer.

4. Do not do anything foolish now that can turn the tables on you. In the end, you will get what you deserve and so will your betrayer. And who knows, if you're fortunate, karma may knock on his or her door.

5. "Revenge is a dish best eaten cold." This old French proverb means vengeance is far more satisfying when it takes place much later than the original offense, if at all.

6. There is no "statute of limitations" on revenge, so it's wise to take the time to see if revenge is really what you need to move forward with your life.

CHAPTER SIX

To Forgive or Not to Forgive, That Is the Question

Holding on to anger is like drinking poison
and expecting the other person to die.
—Unknown

P eople talk about forgiveness, but what does it really mean? As Adam Cohen, researcher on the topic of forgiveness, notes in *Greater Good Magazine*, "Psychologists generally define forgiveness as a conscious, deliberate decision to release feelings of resentment or vengeance toward a person or group who has harmed you, regardless of whether they actually deserve your forgiveness."[24] This decision is about *your* needs, not theirs.

---

24 Cohen, "Research on the Science of Forgiveness: An Annotated Bibliography: Summaries of Research on Forgiveness, Peace, and Well-being."

Given this definition, is forgiveness really necessary? Our stories in this chapter will help you discover which route is best for you.

Through our interviews and research, we have discovered that there are two types of forgiveness. The first is spiritually driven. If forgiving a betrayer helps you attain a peaceful state of mind, then by all means, seek it. For some people, forgiveness of those who have wronged them is a deeply held religious or spiritual value. For others, the spirituality aspect is unnecessary and irrelevant. But moving forward without anger is understood to be a necessary goal in their recovery process. And for others still, forgiveness isn't at all necessary to move on after recovery.

It is essential to note that by forgiving, you are by no means forgetting—nor are you reconciling or excusing the actions of your betrayer. You are simply helping yourself step away from the angry, negative feelings that can drag you down.

Dr. Steven Stosny, a psychologist whose practice includes victims of betrayal, describes forgiveness as "letting go of the hope of having a better past."[25] Doing so can enable you to create a different and better future.

Emotionally, forgiveness helps you heal. It closes the loop on a bad situation, and lets your psyche know it's finally over. José Stevens, PhD, a psychologist and shaman, notes that when you do not forgive someone, you are imprisoning the two of you in the same cell. Forgiveness can help repair a relationship (if that's what you want). And it can help restore your faith and trust in humankind.

This path is perfectly described in Jenny Sanford's moving book, *Staying True,* on her very public betrayal by her ex-husband, former South Carolina governor, Mark Sanford. Jenny sees forgive-

---

25   Stosny, "Anger in the Age of Entitlement. Living and Loving Again. Forgiveness After Betrayal."

ness as necessary for moving forward. She writes:

I reminded myself that it was not my responsibility to mete out judgment. Saying "I forgive you" is not the same as saying "What you have done is okay." If I continued to deny Mark my forgiveness, I would remain entangled in his emotions. I knew I couldn't force myself into his heart by refusing to forgive him. He was supremely self-absorbed … He was not concerned about my feelings. I had become an abstraction to him, an obstacle, and whether I forgave him or not was irrelevant to what he would do next. Forgiveness, then, was for me.[26]

The decision to forgive or not to forgive is based on the needs of the one who was betrayed. For some, like Jenny, there's a deep religious or spiritual need to forgive. For others, that need is less important. So the ultimate decision depends on where you're coming from in life and what *you* need to move forward.

The next two stories provide examples of how and why some can forgive and others cannot.

FORGIVENESS HAS NO "SELL BY" DATE

"Rebecca, did you swipe my ATM card?" asked Carly with all the dispassion she could muster.

"Oh, come on, Carly, why would I do something like that? We're roommates; I could've just asked to borrow some cash. It's gotta be someone else in the dorm."

Reluctantly, Carly chose to believe Rebecca. After all, they had been best friends for almost two years. Having met as freshman at a branch of University of Minnesota, it seemed natural to continue their friendship when they transferred to the Twin Cities campus.

---

26 Sanford, *Staying True.*

Carly packed away her concerns, and the two of them continued their daily routine of classes and activities. But she did notice that the rest of the students in the dorm began pulling away from her. It was subtle, but she felt it. Oh, who knows, *she thought.* Maybe it's all in my imagination.

After Thanksgiving break, Carly discovered more evidence that money was missing from her account. This time, every instinct told her it must have been Rebecca.

Nervously, she confronted Rebecca with her suspicions.

Without missing a beat, Rebecca delivered a wide-eyed response.

"Oh my gosh, money's missing from my account too! Someone's out for both of us, Carly."

Carly felt instant relief.

"Becca, we've got to report this, now."

Over the next few weeks, a female security officer probed the case. Both Rebecca and Carly were asked to submit bank statements. Carly handed everything over immediately, but Rebecca kept giving excuses as to why she couldn't produce the documents.

Finally, the officer returned with a search warrant. Inside Rebecca's desk, she found crudely forged withdrawal form drafts. Clearly Rebecca had many practice attempts at replicating Carly's signature. Under interrogation, Rebecca confessed.

As difficult as it was, Carly followed the security enforcement procedure and took Rebecca to court. Rebecca was convicted and expelled from school.

After Rebecca had been exposed, Carly learned that Rebecca had spread the word that Rebecca was the victim and Carly was the thief. Finally, there was an explanation for Carly's sense of isolation.

But what Carly couldn't explain was the continuing weight of her betrayal by Rebecca. Had Rebecca gotten what she deserved? Had Carly gotten even with her? She knew that because Rebecca had never offered any sign of remorse, forgiveness was impossible. She would just have to forget—and yet she couldn't. Why were her feelings still so raw? Why was it always on her mind?

Five years after these events, Carly ran into Rebecca at a party. Rebecca was highly emotional and visibly shaken as she quietly apologized to Carly.

"I am deeply sorry for deceiving you when you trusted me," she said with downcast eyes.

It was a short conversation, but Carly responded clearly and quickly: "I forgive you."

In that moment, Carly let go of her anger and resentment. And what replaced those negative feelings was forgiveness. It was then that she realized how much more powerful it was to be the forgiver, and how easy it was to shed the weight of her anger about her betrayal.

Carly's ability to forgive Rebecca after her apology is consistent with research that demonstrates a truthful and remorseful apology can quickly turn the tide of anger and desire for revenge into a feeling of forgiveness. It is important to note that Carly did not excuse Rebecca for her betrayal of trust. She simply and graciously accepted her apology for behaving badly.

Even in medical malpractice cases, when the offending physician apologizes in an honest way, the outcome of the case is significantly more positive. A recent article in the November 2018 *National Law Review* notes that events with medical errors were resolved by apology alone in 43 percent of the cases—an amazing fact that underscores the power of forgiveness.[27]

Now it's time for Tracey's story, one in which forgiveness seemed impossible until the very end.

---

27   Ackerman, "You Had Me at 'I'm Sorry': The Impact of Physicians' Apologies of Medical Malpractice Litigation."

DEMONS AND DENIAL

Charles had a history of evil behavior. Even as a child, he tormented his younger sister.

"Don't push me!" Tracey screamed, as Charles tossed her into the laundry chute.

"You poured motor oil in the fish tank, you creep!" Tracey yelled at her brother.

"Don't! Please don't do this!" Tracey cried as he pinned her in front of an open window on the second floor of their home.

Tracey constantly looked to her stern German nanny to protect her because neither one of her parents believed her stories. Fortunately, her nanny did her best to protect her, but her nanny was not always around.

As the firstborn son, Charles could do no wrong, and Tracey was just a "silly girl." In order to protect herself, Tracey developed her own skills to deflect Charles's aggressiveness.

As they both grew to adolescence, the battles became more intense. The attacks escalated. Near strangulation and setting fire to her bed were simply part of torture that Charles and his friend had in store for a teenaged Tracey.

One day after school, high on heroin, the boys forced Tracey to drink Scotch whiskey. After getting her drunk, her brother watched as his friend attempted to rape her. Amazingly, Tracey fought them both off. She escaped and called the police.

When Tracey's mother came home that day, she was appalled—not by Charles's actions, but by the fact that Tracey had called the police.

"Once again, you overreacted," her mother scolded. "And this dirty laundry is out for everyone to see."

Now it was Tracey's turn to be appalled. She knew her mother didn't like to discuss "unhappy subjects," but she flat-out ignored the fact that her daughter's welfare was being severely jeopardized. Clearly, her mother was guilty of betraying a basic trust between a parent and a child.

This pattern of denial concerning Charles's behavior helped her parents miss his escalating deep dive into drugs. Even as several of his friends died horrific deaths from car crashes while driving impaired, Tracey's parents talked about the tragedies and bad luck, blind to the reality.

Tracey finally grew up, went into therapy to address and move forward from her many family betrayals, and moved away from her dysfunctional family. She graduated from college, married, and made a meaningful life for herself. Although she remained distant from her family, after her parents' death, she chose to take on the tragic duty of caring for Charles, her dying brother, who by fifty-three had been destroyed by a life of drugs and alcohol.

For the first time in his life, Charles apologized to Tracey for the pain he had caused. Despite his apology, Tracey was unable to forgive him. Her brother's abuse had gone on too long, the hurt was too deep, and she was convinced it was another one of his classic attempts at manipulation.

Tracey also helped to care for Charles's son while Charles was in the hospital. She decided to bring her children to say goodbye to their uncle so they could bear witness to the destructive effect drugs had had on his unhappy life.

Talking with the doctors, Tracey finally came to understand that her brother's addiction was a sickness. The abusive behaviors were out of his control. Only after many years of rage did Tracey forgive Charles. She shut down the anger, realizing her brother was a broken person, and gave her children an important life lesson.

Granting Charles forgiveness before his death allowed her to move on. While she never absolved her brother of his heinous behavior, she arrived at a place where she could think about some of the good times they'd shared, without the shadow of anger constantly hanging over her head.

Both Carly and Tracey chose to forgive their betrayers.

This was not a feasible path for either Richard or Miranda in the following stories.

A FRIENDSHIP DESTRUCTS

In the lobby of the Beverly Hills Hotel, a scene had erupted.

Two college-aged guys were blind drunk and going after each other.

Jake glared at his former best friend and softly said, "You know, Hailey and I are sleeping together."

Richard snapped his head and came back with, "Well, so are we."

An evil smile crossed Jake's face as he said loudly, "No Richard, not any more. You're done. History. Total history."

Richard was slack-jawed.

Jake repeated his words, each time turning up the volume and watching the audience around them grow. He felt woozily triumphant, even as the security guard wrestled him out of the lobby and threw him into a cab.

Richard and Jake's incident had its roots in a private school both had attended on Chicago's North Shore. It was a place of too much money and too little parenting, where Jake had easily secured his position as golden boy.

It was as much a surprise to Richard as it was to everyone else that Jake had chosen him as his best friend and wingman. Richard enjoyed his popularity from Jake's reflected glory, just as Jake enjoyed the protection of Richard's unquestioning loyalty.

Hailey was part of the mix because she was Richard's girlfriend. Her contribution to the group was an edgy wit and a troubled past that was truly intriguing. Richard was very protective of Hailey, as she was his first love. After each went their own way to college, Richard and Hailey continued their relationship despite geographic separation, making an effort to get together whenever possible.

Jake dropped out of college after one year and returned home with a heavy cocaine habit. But Hey, *he thought.* With all this money and no place to go, I might as well get high.

Soon, the cozy trio became toxic.

Unbeknownst to Richard, Jake and Hailey became lovers. Richard blew up when Hailey confessed. He confronted Jake. He confronted Hailey. But they had both betrayed him. He tried to be a bigger person, but the deception undid him.

Cheating, reuniting, and taunting Richard became a regular emotional game for Hailey and Jake. The fight at the hotel was the final death knell for Richard and Jake's already tenuous friendship.

Later, when Jake discovered Hailey was seeing another of his best friends, he came to Richard for sympathy and support. Jake apologized and asked forgiveness for his past actions. He knew now what it was like to feel the anger and despair that Richard had lived through. But forgiveness was not in the cards. Richard could never forget Jake's treachery, and he was now secure enough to confidently walk away from this destructive relationship. The emotional damage to Jake allowed Richard to move forward and put his anger aside. In many ways, refusing forgiveness was Richard's revenge.

And now, Miranda's story exemplifies the betrayal of trust at its most basic level ... and at its worst:

A FATHER'S INEXCUSABLE ACTS

Miranda was blinded by Randy from the beginning; he was fifteen years her senior, rich, and loads of fun. She was thrilled when he started paying attention to her after her cousin had ended her relationship with him.

"I couldn't deal with his little lies," her cousin, Logan, told her.

"Minor stuff," Miranda responded. "I mean, he's a catch."

Miranda was enamored of Randy's life: how he ran a successful family business, had graduated from MIT, and was a captain in the Army Reserve.

After they married, she found out he that frequented sex clubs in the city. She asked about this, but when he told her he was doing it only at the request of his clients, she shrugged it off, thinking it wasn't up to her to judge where and when he entertained clients and business prospects. After all, he was the CEO and the business was profitable, so clearly, he was making the right judgment calls.

Children came quickly, first James, then Chloe. Miranda was in awe of Randy's close relationships with their children; he was so loving and attentive. Randy always wanted to read them stories before bed and snuggle with them before they fell asleep. And when Chloe had nightmares, Randy would leap out of bed to soothe her.

The only blip came when Miranda announced her third pregnancy.

"Get an abortion or get a divorce," he said.

She defied him. Alexander was born, and Randy quickly relented and became as involved with Alexander as with the other children.

Life continued and all seemed good. But as the children were growing up, she and Randy were increasingly isolated as a couple.

Asking her friends why they no longer wanted to get together, one told her honestly that Randy was too "touchy" and made women uncomfortable. She also told Miranda how inappropriate Richard's behavior had become with his constant patter of sexually laden remarks. And she emphasized, "everyone" felt this way. But Miranda was always welcome—alone, with or without her children—and her friends still cared about her. Miranda was upset, but decided that her husband's style wouldn't change, so it made no sense to talk with him about this. She would see her friends during the day and on "girls' nights out."

And when her friends refused to allow their children in the house if Miranda wasn't present, she looked the other way, and chalked it up to parents who misunderstood Randy's natural warmth and affection. Perhaps, she thought. They are just jealous of the fact that, unlike other husbands, Randy is always delighted to take care of the children.

Growing up, the children had bouts of dislike for their father. Chloe insisted on saying, "He's not my father; he's Randy."

Concerned, Miranda arranged for the children to see a psychiatrist. All he could pry out of them was that their father was weird. Then the children refused to return to the psychiatrist, and Miranda simply assumed each child was going through a phase that would soon resolve itself. She told them that it was their decision, and when none of them mentioned dislike for their father again, she believed that all was now fine.

But one night, when Chloe was a teen, studying with her boyfriend in her room, Miranda became upset that the door was closed. She demanded that they study in the kitchen or he needed to leave.

"Mom, do you really think I'd fool around in that bed?" Chloe asked. "That's the bed Randy molests me in, and he's been doing it since I was five." Miranda froze, trying to process what she had just heard.

Chloe begged Miranda not to tell anyone or do anything about it.

"Daddy will hate me! My brothers will hate me!" Chloe pleaded.

Miranda's shock was monumental. She immediately called Randy's uncle, who told her to believe her daughter.

"Unfortunately, my dear, you've discovered our family's dark secret. And it's something no one really wants to discuss. Just believe Chloe and *watch out for your sons. Call your lawyer immediately and kick Randy out. Now."*

Miranda was in a state of disbelief. "What kind of animal would sexually abuse his kid? Not my husband," she repeated to herself.

The next day, much to Miranda's surprise, Chloe decided to go to school. Midmorning, the phone rang.

A tearful Chloe said, "Mom, I can't hide it anymore. I want to tell my counselor. Please meet me in her office in twenty minutes." She hung up before Miranda could respond.

The counselor was reasonable and empathetic, but also resolute in her response.

"There is no way around this. It is incest. Children do not lie about this, and we are required by law to call the police." The counselor put Miranda on notice: if she did not act immediately to remove Randy from the house, she would be in danger of losing her children for not protecting them.

Miranda's next step was finding a lawyer and having a restraining order issued. Randy contested it, saying, "I never did anything against anyone's will." Hearing his protestations, a brave but emotionally devastated Miranda no longer had any doubt.

Divorce and court-mandated distance did not heal the serious wounds.

Chloe survived a yearlong hospitalization, and emerged with a desire to move forward in her life. She is now in college and still under the constant care of a therapist. She wants to become a psychologist and help abused children.

The boys remained angry with Miranda for taking their father away. James refused to admit he had been molested. But both Miranda and Chloe believe that he had been. Randy continued to try to buy forgiveness by sending all three children expensive gifts, including cars. To this day, it has not worked.

Miranda finally pieced together the many small and large data points and saw the truth of her husband's involvement with her children. She must live with the guilt of her blind trust in the goodness and innocence of paternal love. She now recognizes the ugliness in Randy's unusual attention to the children, and her friends' attempts to wave the red flags that she'd rationalized or simply ignored.

For Miranda, forgiveness is not an option. Not only did Randy refuse to admit any responsibility, he committed horrific acts of sexual violence against her children.

Remember his chilling words, "I never did anything against anyone's will." That vicious, self-serving belief and stunning lack of remorse prohibits forgiveness from ever happening.

Here are Miranda's own words:

"Knowing my daughter, and probably my son also, will struggle for the rest of their lives means I can never forgive Randy. I am enraged and horribly sad, and I always will be. If he apologized and acknowledged what a horrendous act occurred, Chloe and I could possibly forgive his betrayal of everything a parent should do and be, but we could still never forget. His refusal to take ownership for his horrendous actions and behavior means he is never worthy of our forgiveness. In our situation, it is possible to move forward without forgiveness. While we may never be able to seal off his actions, knowing that he truly doesn't care about her allows me to move forward. It needs to be about her, not about him."

As Dr. Stosny notes, to increase the possibility of forgiveness, betrayers need to:

1. Fully embrace one's responsibilities for actions.

2. Understand the pain and suffering that has been caused and experienced.

3. Recognize how long it can take the betrayed to heal (sometimes, it's a matter of years, not months).

4. Discover and show empathy to the one betrayed throughout the recovery process.

5. Accept the fact that there's now a change in the power dynamic and the betrayer has lost power.

6. Realize that complete trust may never be granted and cannot be demanded.[28]

Sometimes, it's possible to create a new future for both the betrayer and the betrayed. But that decision belongs to the person betrayed alone. To increase the possibility of a shared future, the betrayer needs to show remorse, sorrow, empathy, and vulnerability. The betrayed needs to heal and develop defense mechanisms that ensure a pattern of betrayal won't litter the future. It is also important that the betrayed develops wise trust with small tests of honesty to ensure the new potential future can flourish.

Forgiveness, despite what many believe, is not a spiritual or religious decision that lets the betrayer off the hook. Instead, it is simply finding a way to free yourself from the emotional pain that can force you into an eternal dance with your betrayer. So acknowledge the pain and validate it; do not fall into the trap of endlessly reliving the pain anew because that will slow your healing process and allow resentment and rage to creep back into your life.

As John Haney and Leslie Hardie, therapists for betrayed spouses, have wisely noted, "If forgiveness does not occur, it can really mean that the betrayed person is 'forever choosing' to allow another's

---

28 Stosny, "Anger in the Age of Entitlement. Living and Loving Again. Forgiveness After Betrayal."

hurtful actions to live 'rent-free' in their life forever."[29]

Dr. Stosny, the therapist we mentioned earlier, takes this notion one step further. He sees forgiveness as putting your emotional house in order instead of holding a grudge or punishing the betrayer. Personal detachment can set you on a path to well-being, and get you ready to say, "I can put this all behind me."

Keep in mind that forgiveness is not the first step; it is the last step in a process of healing. As both Stosny and Dickenson note, the emotional milestones that can lead to forgiveness include:

1. Regaining control of your emotions and personal healing through self-care and compassion.

2. Developing a balanced view of the relationship in which the betrayer can be seen as more than the embodiment of evil. After all, you would not have trusted that person if they were totally evil and had no positive attributes.

3. Restoring your ability to believe that it is possible to trust others.

4. Putting the rage and anger behind you.

5. Putting the situation into the past and out of the present. This is not forgetting, but rather, resetting your focus and attention.

6. And finally ... forgiving ... or not.

If you truly believe that forgiveness is crucial to moving on with your life, then it needs to happen. If not, you're entirely free to give it a pass, and, as Dr. José Stevens has suggested, move out of your own way and stop being the obstacle to your future. Your future is waiting for you to create it anew.

---

29 Haney, "Psychotherapeutic Considerations for Working With Betrayed Spouses: A Four-Task Recovery Model."

So we now know that honest remorse, while not a guarantee, can invite forgiveness, but how sorry is sorry enough? Extensive research by Julie Fitness, professor at Macquarie University, and author of "Betrayal, Rejection, Revenge, and Forgiveness: An Interpersonal Script Approach," focuses on types of forgiveness after spousal betrayal.[30]

She finds that the difference between the situations where the betrayer was forgiven and those where the betrayer was not is simple. Is this a first-time occurrence or a repeat performance? More than one betrayal can indicate a serious lack of regret, and can be viewed as proof the betrayer never loved their spouse.

Even true remorse was not always seen as reason enough to forgive. The breakdown of trust for some can never be mended. Even when forgiven, 75 percent of the betrayed spouses meted out punishments as ongoing reminders.

Here's a stunning fact: 70 percent of unforgiven partners' punishments were acts of revenge, including such actions as physical abuse, destruction of possessions, abandonment, and denunciation of family and friends. This just goes to prove Hell hath no fury like a spouse scorned.

Fitness further notes the following:

> Both revenge and repeatedly reminding [the spouse of the betrayer] were reportedly motivated by the betrayed party's need to communicate the depth of their hurt or to regain some power in the relationship—to feel "one-up" relative to the partner. ... For victims of betrayal, reminders appear to serve at least three purposes: fine-tuning the degree of mutual suffering, readjusting the balance of power, and behavioral deterrence. ... Convincing partners in the

---

30 Fitness, "Betrayal, Rejection, Revenge, and Forgiveness: An Interpersonal Script Approach."

aftermath of betrayal that they are, in fact, cherished, requires considerable effort and persistence on the part of remorseful offenders, especially if trust is to ever be fully restored.

Based on Fitness's research and the perspectives of our survivors, each person betrayed needs to determine for him or herself whether or not forgiveness is necessary and feasible.

Once again, forgiveness is about moving past the anger, not about understanding and accepting the betrayal or condoning the betrayer. It is a jumping off point to look past the faults and actions of the betrayer and to recast the relationship: moving forward with it or halting it.

Here's a possible road map:

1. Create a safe space to think.

2. Isolate and limit the time you devote to reliving, reviewing, and retelling the betrayal in all its nasty detail.

3. Decide if you think it is necessary to forgive, or wall it off and put it behind you.

4. Determine what you need from your betrayer to even consider the possibility of forgiveness.

5. Establish whether you need to revenge this act of betrayal in order to move forward.

6. Do not ask others for advice. Listen to your heart as to how best to move forward.

7. If revenge is important, clearly consider its consequences and unanticipated consequences on your future, your self-esteem, and your morals.

The point of all this is to understand that forgiveness benefits the forgiver more than the forgiven, and the betrayed more than the betrayer, because it means letting go of the betrayal and liberating yourself.

In our next chapter, we will move further up the path to your new future by considering the secret sauce that makes it all possible—resilience.

TAKEAWAYS

1. Forgiveness is not a one-time event. It's an ongoing process that evolves over time. It means letting the pain of betrayal go, but it doesn't mean forgetting.

2. Stop letting betrayal torture you with sleepless nights. Make a choice to unilaterally forgive or not to forgive, and occupy your mind with thoughts about your future, not your past.

3. Forgiveness isn't a short-term goal; it's the final part of the recovery process. It's about regaining control of your emotional well-being as a step in moving forward.

4. Forgiveness will help you far more than the betrayer; it's a gift you give yourself.

5. Ending a traumatic relationship, once you swim through the pain, can be positive, because it's focused on you—not the betrayer.

6. Forgiveness enables you to regain the power that was taken from you. You are the only person who can grant forgiveness and the only person who can refuse to provide it.

7. Sometimes forgiveness is just not possible. If you can move forward without it, then that is fine too.

CHAPTER SEVEN

Resilience—What Doesn't Kill You Makes You Stronger

He who laughs, lasts.
—Mary Pettibone Poole

Life is not a matter of holding good cards,
but of playing a poor hand well.
—Robert Louis Stevenson

I n previous chapters, we've walked through the choices you have after being betrayed. How will you survive that moment of betrayal? Will you seek revenge? Will you grant forgiveness? Will you never forgive but try to forget? Or will you just wallow in the betrayal, hoping for a different past, drowning in shame and humiliation, and afraid to ever trust again?

We discovered the true key to unlocking a new and better future is a superpower called resilience: that ability in each of us to survive, and to position ourselves to go forward.

The American Psychological Association defines resilience as "the process of adapting well in the face of adversity, trauma, tragedy, threats, or significant sources of stress ... It means 'bouncing back' from difficult experiences."[31]

General George S. Patton describes it best: "I don't measure a man's success by how high he climbs the ladder, but how high he bounces when he hits bottom."

Is there a secret to bouncing higher? To paraphrase author Abigail Trafford's wise observations in her excellent book, *Crazy Time*:

> Betrayal is smack in the middle of the failure of the past to live up to your expectations. Resilience allows you to maneuver between the two and enables you *to change and to grow*. For some, after the initial phase of high drama and telling everyone the story of how they were betrayed, resilience takes the form of psychological withdrawal. Literally a phase of hibernation where, to survive, it becomes necessary to pull inward and block out the world. During this period, one's life, hopes, values, and an ability to trust are examined and evaluated. The luxury and pain of what was lost can finally be permitted.[32]

This cozy state of withdrawal allows you time for introspection, and helps you get a realistic view of what happened without internalizing the bad stuff, like blame. It's a cocoon from which you can reach out to others for support and kick-start your recovery.

Resilience is more than "adapting" to a situation. It's withstanding

---

31 American Psychological Association, "The Road to Resilience."
32 Trafford, *Crazy Time*.

the pressures of betrayal and moving ahead with renewed strength.

Jenny was a young woman who felt she'd lost everything. The only things she had left were her self-respect and survival instincts, which were exactly what she needed to move on.

LOVE IS BLIND

It was a scene straight out of Downton Abbey, *where Edith was left alone at the altar, only this was not a long-running BBC series.*

This was Jenny and Devin's wedding. Jenny's altar and, astoundingly, Jenny's missing groom.

Devin had disappeared and Jenny was horrified and mortified. As her father led her out of the church and into a waiting car, she felt her heart explode. How could this have happened?

As Jenny recovered in the arms of her family and friends, she began to piece together certain odd behaviors of Devin. Behaviors that she thought were simply a unique but harmless part of his idiosyncratic personality. Behaviors that she had learned to accept as "simply Devin."

Yes, he was overly critical of her, but she thought that it was his way of pushing her to be her best self. After all, he constantly called out her lack of confidence and used her unwillingness to push back at him as evidence.

And yes, he was flippant about their future.

"If our marriage doesn't work out," he said when they had small disagreements. "We'll just get a divorce." But he always laughed when he said it, and she knew that he shared her belief that marriage is forever.

And, yes, Jenny was irked by Devin's refusal to ever show up on time. Here, too, she saw it as his way of trying to make her less controlling and more flexible as a way to reduce her stress. And anyway, should her compulsion to always be on time be more important than his need to have some freedom around arbitrary timelines?

For three weeks after her humiliation at the altar, Jenny tried her best to take care of herself. She spent time with friends, treated herself to a daily massage, and tried to concentrate on reading books and watching movies—anything to keep Devin out of her mind. Finally, she felt ready to start to get her life back in order.

As she sat at her desk reviewing recent bills, she opened a bank statement from her joint account with Devin. It was the one detail she had neglected to take care of.

This was impossible. He couldn't have. But he did.

The day of the planned wedding, Devin had bled the account and withdrawn all the money.

Jenny quickly went to check the room where she had insisted that all the wedding presents be stored out of sight, until she had the strength to begin the process of returning them.

Many gifts that they had opened together were missing. And most disconcerting, all the wedding checks that had been sent to their apartment were gone.

Ever the dutiful ex-fiancée, she texted both sets of parents the startling news. All the parents wanted to begin criminal proceedings against Devin to have him return all that he had stolen. For Jenny, the only thing that mattered, however, was the theft of her heart. She had no interest in facing him and pressing charges, and so she begged them to let him go. She did not want to ever see or hear from, or about, him again.

It took Jenny a very long time to redevelop trust in people. But with the steady advice of a sound therapist, she came to understand the destructive nature of Devin and the ways that her trust and constant rationalizations for his behavior had prevented her from seeing the red flags.

Fortunately, Jenny's betrayal happened at a young age, and, over time, she has grown to understand her future was much better off without Devin.

Jenny was blinded by the power of love. That was the root of her betrayal. But how many of us have looked behind the curtain of true love to honestly assess what's behind it? Years later, Jenny realized she had been too willing to assume responsibility and rationalize Devin's faults as her faults, and, as a result, she'd missed all the red flags. Throughout their relationship she had let him steadily hammer away at her self-esteem. As painful as the experience was, with the help of friends and family, she moved forward and discovered her true value.

She now realizes that Devin's betrayal was truly the best wedding gift possible.

Next is Nancy's story. It shows how strength and resilience helped her carve out a powerful new path after being betrayed by her husband of forty years. When interviewed, Nancy said, "I will now describe the ashes from which I have arisen. I am the phoenix of my life." Her attitude is the epitome of resilience.

THE PHOENIX RISES

"Nancy, I'm not interested in sex," Tom, her husband, said flatly. He rolled away from her to turn off the light and continued, "I mean, it's obvious to everyone you've let yourself go." She withered in shame.

Nancy woke up the next day and saw the check he'd left for the month's expenses. How were three kids under ten and two adults supposed to live on that? Well, she decided, if she was really careful, it could be done. And if she didn't, Tom would lapse into one of his sullen and volatile moods, which were even worse than being criticized for not staying within budget.

Instinctively, Nancy knew none of her friends would believe that Tom, her high-flying, fabulously successful, investment banker husband could be so controlling and cheap. That's why she kept all these injustices to herself. Including his constant reminders that she had lost her intellectual edge. Despite the fact that she had graduated summa cum laude from an Ivy League school and he had struggled in a third-tier one, she accepted his assessment. And, looking in the mirror, she also believed his disparaging remarks about her lost attractiveness.

Nancy's denial allowed her to justify to herself that his job was highly stressful and that time would get the relationship back on track. And if she could just look the other way during this seemingly never-ending difficult period, it would all magically revert way back to their happy-couple period.

As their life progressed through the years, it continued to look idyllic from the outside. They owned a beautiful farm in Western Massachusetts, which was a haven from their hectic New York City home life, and a perfect retreat for her and her children when Tom was too busy with work to join them.

Time went on, and the children were on the path to adulthood. Then, Tom was offered a job that involved a significant amount of travel to Europe. She was dismayed to realize that she was relieved at the thought of his extended absences.

Once again, Nancy broached the subject of money before Tom left for six weeks.

"More money," he said. "If you want more money, get a job. Not my problem."

He finished packing and left for the airport.

After years of being told she was worthless, Nancy marshaled her inner forces, and decided to do exactly what he suggested. She would not simply "get a job;" she would create a job. Through her volunteer work, she knew that she was skilled at putting together fundraising events, and she truly loved the work. She then contacted everyone she knew, and created a business as an independent event planner. In a short period of time, she had a roster of clients and was on the road to success. And she finally had some money of her own to spend as she wished.

As always, Tom disparaged her, calling her company a silly, time-wasting hobby and ignoring her ability to build a truly successful business. Despite his attacks, Nancy reveled in her newfound confidence and realized that between her business, her friends, her children, and her relaxing weekends, she enjoyed the new rhythm of her life without Tom's constant disapproval—a rhythm that was abruptly dispelled upon each and every one of Tom's returns. Each time he returned, it appeared that his attacks on her competence were heightened. He continued to refuse to acknowledge the value of the business she was building. Or how she had raised the children with little input from him. Or the friendships and social life she had formed on her own. Nancy was constantly torn between his hateful dismissal of her abilities and the reality that she was finally building her own inner strength.

Despite her growing self-confidence and independence, she still had the fantasy that once he retired, they would be a loving couple again. She believed that as his career wound down toward retirement, he would repent and they would reignite the relationship she so desperately wanted. That was why, for their fortieth anniversary, Nancy was willing and happy to buy Tom an exorbitantly expensive Swiss watch that he coveted. She hoped that he would see how much she still cared and would redis-cover the love he felt for her.

It took only one voicemail message to explode her self-delusion.

"Hello, this is CVS, and I'm sorry, but your insurance won't cover the Viagra prescription your husband submitted."

In a flash, Nancy knew Tom was cheating, because their sex life had evaporated over ten years ago. As she swam through her misery at this overt betrayal of her love and trust, and became less emotional, she started to critically review Tom's behavior over the past few years. Why was he constantly on the phone during their son's wedding weekend? What were those long absences about? Why did he care less and less about his family?

The answer lay in a poorly hidden stash of printed emails Nancy discovered at the farm. It was not a woman Tom was involved with, but a Frenchman named Henri. While Nancy supported everyone's right to choose their sexual partners, her support did not extend to her husband's affair.

It took her some time to process this information, but Nancy, using her own money, hired a private investigator to confirm the emails. Unbeknownst to Tom, the investigator followed him on his next business trip to France and took photos for Nancy. The final betrayal was when she saw her anniversary gift—that expensive watch—on Henri's wrist. The very same watch that Tom had recently mentioned that he was afraid he had misplaced, and asked her to call the insurance company and get the process started, just in case it was lost.

Nancy had finally had enough. She hired a tough-minded divorce lawyer and began to protect her business assets as well as monies that her parents had left in a trust.

The denouement occurred when Tom returned to the farm, busy with plans to add on to their century-old building.

Nancy put dinner on the table and said, "We shouldn't do the addition because our marriage is unlikely to survive. I know about Henri and I am unwilling to stay married to someone who cheats and has hidden the fact that he is gay. And by the way, claiming the loss of a watch that you gave a as gift to someone is insurance fraud!"

"What are you talking about?" Tom spit out. He jumped up from the table and locked himself in a bedroom. He came out the next day and begged her to give their marriage another chance.

Nancy knew at once, there would never be another chance. This final betrayal of her never-ending trust was the tipping point for her.

The shock of the extent of Tom's deception provided Nancy the ability to realize her husband's actions were calculated to undermine her self-worth and increase his control over her. And, she also had to admit that she was a willing participant in her own destruction. His power over her made Nancy ignore all the red flags that signaled her husband's betrayal, one that began shortly after they were married and continued for years through the never-ending drip, drip, drip of demeaning comments and irrational demands.

As Nancy explains, "I didn't know the person I had become. I kept looking the other way and kept my concerns and feelings to myself because I didn't know that I had any options. When I complained about the way he treated me, he told me that if I was unhappy I should leave, but I would never get a penny, as the money was all his. Because I didn't want to discuss what was happening with anyone, I did not try to determine if he was telling the truth. I had never heard of community property, and stupidly, I never researched the laws about divorce and finances. I guess it was because I did not want to know the truth about him."

As we discussed in Chapter Two and Chapter Three, a critical step for the betrayer is to dehumanize and demean the soon-to-be-betrayed subject. Tom's process of betrayal began early in their marriage, by robbing Nancy of her self-esteem and identity. He betrayed her trust despite saying he would always have her best interest at heart.

Against these odds, Nancy made a clean break. Fortunately, her inner strength was eroded but not destroyed, and her "bounce" began when she started her own business and discovered that she could be successful in doing something that she loved. She is now leading the life she created, desires, and deserves. She has a thriving career, loving adult children, and travels the world. Every new day is living proof of her resilience, self-confidence, and value. And Tom? Tom suffered karmic revenge. He was fired from his job for a small theft shortly before retirement. Henri left Tom for a more attractive option. His children hate him for his constant indifference and emotional abuse of their mother.

As Nancy says, "He is completely alone. His funeral reception could be held in a phone booth." For Nancy, forgiveness came in the form of moving past her anger about the number of years she trusted in Tom and waited for his love. As she notes, "At the end of the day, I am thriving while he is barely surviving. Letting go of my anger in light of this rebalancing was easy."

This next story is about Phyllis, another amazing phoenix, who rose from the ashes.

A WORLD OF PORN, PRIVILEGE, AND DECEIT

Phyllis opened a closet and discovered yet another stash of her husband's porn collection. Teddy and his maddening interest in photos of naked ladies was the only stain on their otherwise happy marriage.

Phyllis and Teddy were a good match from the start. Married for thirty-five years, they were a team who loved life. Friends admired their kinetic energy, and at times, seemed envious of their smooth marital road. Early on, Phyllis knew about Ted's proclivities, but put it in the back of her mind. Growing up in a family of all women, she believed all men were into this kind of thing, and it made no sense to blow up a fantastic marriage for such an isolated obsession. After all, they not only were spouses, but each other's best friends. They had made an early decision to never have children so they could always focus on each other. And Phyllis agreed, early on, that she would be the income earner while he pursued his passion as an artist. Part of her willingness to do so was the knowledge that his father had committed a significant trust to be paid to Teddy upon his father's death.

Phyllis saw herself as sophisticated, above petty judgments. She was a powerful and successful senior executive who held a PhD in psychology, no less.

Thirty years into their marriage, she had a wake-up call when she discovered Teddy on a popular "sugar daddy" site, where women listed their financial needs and promised "anything" in return to men who could provide financial help. Taken aback, she questioned him as to what in the world he was doing.

"Oh, come on, Phyl, I heard about the site and was intrigued. You're a psychologist. Aren't you fascinated by the premise also? I'm just exploring; there's no harm in that," he laughed. "Besides," he teased. "Then I can have company when you travel."

But then he admitted he was eager to meet other women—"but just to meet them," he swore to her. "I don't want a relationship with anyone but you. We are perfect, as always."

Phyllis knew, unchecked, his predilection could snowball. That's why they reached out to a counselor. Teddy was duly apologetic and Phyllis accepted his genuine remorse. He promised, "Never again. I'm done with those sites." So, Phyllis pushed her fears aside. Nothing had really happened, and he was being open with her. Teddy and their marriage were just too good to give up.

Worried that there was some sexual need that she wasn't fulfilling, she even went to a sexual body retreat to amp up their love life. She was desperately willing to take responsibility for his actions.

But trouble bubbled up again two years later. As Phyllis was printing out an expense receipt on Teddy's computer, she found an email from a woman in Washington DC, describing their upcoming weekend together.

So, this was the reason he'd rushed down there for repairs on their condo! She tried to call him, but he didn't answer his phone. She then called his best friend, who said that they had been together all weekend, and asked why was she asking about another woman.

When Teddy returned, Phyllis confronted him. After all the discussions, and all his promises, how could he even think about a secret affair, let alone have one?

"Look, why can't I meet someone and have a great conversation and some fun?" he asked. "I promise: this is the first time and the only woman I have met. And we never had sex; I wouldn't do that to you."

Phyllis demanded his phone.

When Teddy handed her his phone, she saw innumerable texts that proved he was not only dating this one woman, but was deeply involved with several other women. And there was sex. Lots of it.

Devastated and bewildered, Phyllis realized she had been lied to for over eight years. She immediately decamped to her sister's house, where her sister convinced her that seeing an attorney would be a good idea.

A cascade of betrayals soon came to light. Teddy had been spending tens of thousands of dollars on his affairs. He had even been bringing women to their home for trysts whenever she traveled. He'd been having sex with them in her own bed, and all the while, had remained on the lookout for newer, better, and younger women. And this was all done through cash withdrawals from their joint checking account—an account that she trusted him to manage.

Another confrontation revealed a contrary and unrepentant Teddy.

"I've been doing research, and I really do believe I'm polyamorous," he explained. "I'm sure you have heard about this sexual need. It's the practice of, and desire for, intimate relationships with more than one partner. It's not my fault; it's just the way I'm wired. You wouldn't be mad at me if I told you that I had diabetes, would you?"

She was destroyed by his admission and attitude. How could she have missed this side of him over the many long years of what she had always considered a wonderful marriage? He'd betrayed everything that she believed in. Despite her desire to crawl in a hole and die, Phyllis decided to tell family and friends the sordid details of what was happening. Physically weakened, she began running marathons to get her though these devastating realizations.

Teddy's sister, who Phyllis viewed as dearly as her own sister, dealt another blow.

"He's truly enlightened for being so honest with you. I mean, it takes real courage to recognize one's true self," Mary proclaimed. "But don't worry, he wants to stay married. You'll eventually learn to understand his needs and it will all work out just fine. And if you divorce, you won't get a penny of the family money."

Yes, *Phyllis thought,* and it takes real courage to betray the trust of your wife who has supported your artistic career and never asked for your help in paying bills. *For all the years of their marriage, Teddy, the artist, had held out his future inheritance as his right not to work for salary, but to instead pursue his art.*

It became clear to Phyllis that despite the fact that she had a successful high-level career as a public-sector executive, she had ceded her identity to the marriage. Without her marriage to Teddy, she believed, she was nothing. When Teddy begged for forgiveness, she actually tried to believe it was possible, but then she finally recognized that she could never accept Teddy's request for a polyamorous relationship. It was absurd. And finally, the revelation came: she deserved far more than that. She told Teddy that divorce was the only option.

Having worked through a very painful year with PTSD-like symptoms, Phyllis left Teddy and is slowly recovering. She discovered that, unlike his family, her friends were equally angry about his betrayal, and closed ranks around her to protect her.

Unfortunately, there were multiple betrayals, and the financial betrayal hurt her in many ways too. She discovered that, counting all the years of their marriage, he had spent hundreds of thousands of dollars on his "women friends." So while it was tempting to ask for a leave of absence from her job, Phyllis found the deep dive back into her professional life, and the income that it brought, to be a lifeline, essential to rebuilding her emotional strength.

Today, Teddy is happily surfing the web to find new dates. Phyllis has bounced back higher with a recent promotion and an ability to think about her life without anger. Also, she summoned the strength to sue Teddy for the monies that were promised for "their" retirement. And recently, she has recorded her best time ever in a marathon.

Just like Nancy, Phyllis had blindly trusted in a flawed spouse and a flawed marital relationship. Because so much of her self-identity was wrapped up in the relationship, when he fell apart, she needed to dive deep to fully discover her self-worth and ability to become independent. In doing so, like Nancy, she discovered her own deep well of resilience in the face of her world blowing up around her. The clear realization that only she could put it back together was transformative, but it didn't happen overnight. She allowed herself over a year to grieve for all she lost. She can now celebrate rediscovering her powerful and confident self.

As Phyllis notes, "It was easier for me to move forward, because, even though I was betrayed by the person I trusted most in this world, knowing he was the betrayer and I had acted fully ethically and honestly in all my dealings gave me a clear conscience. What happened at the end was his 'fault' due to his flaws, traits, and characteristics. Sure, some of it may have been preventable, had I been more aware and attuned to his behaviors, but I loved him and was blind to all that. But, I exited knowing this was not a person I cared to interact with anymore. I finally found that I could define myself without him. I had built my professional success on my own. And I realized my future was there for me to define and enjoy. He could not take that from me."

Phyllis's only regret is the impact of the financial betrayal. That's why she is holding firm in her lawsuit, unwilling to cave under pressure from Teddy and his family to settle. When asked if the lawsuit is a form of revenge, Phyllis is clear:

"It's not revenge when you seek to receive all that has been promised and is due to you. The lawsuit is actually a formal statement of the value that I brought to our marriage. It's my return on my investment."

Emily's story is next. It's the betrayal of a corporate advisor, and while it may not be as emotionally charged as the previous betrayals, it is still a powerful narrative of resilience, with a delightful touch of karma.

STEELY RESILIENCE THAT TURNED INTO PURE GOLD

Two words captured it all: sabotage and betrayal. Emily had just learned that her board of directors had hired a consultancy to assess her competence.

That's right, her board. She was the CEO. She was the one whose family had poured years of their lives into this business. Emily looked in the mirror and wondered how she had come to this point.

It all began when the family decided that the needs of the family and the business would be best served if it was acquired by a bigger company. They had built a solid, safe, and—most importantly—profitable company, but now they felt it was time to sell. To accomplish this, they were introduced to Darryl, who was recommended by their accountant as someone who could guide the family through the sale. He was an experienced deal guy, with a solid track record that everyone agreed could be put to good use in protecting their interests.

"Hey, all you Millers, I've been doing some thinking. After digging into the company's records, I believe there's a bigger opportunity here. Why not consider taking the business public? Build it into an even more valuable entity," he proposed. "That would be a fabulous legacy to give to your daughter."

Her family was impressed and they bought into the idea. It was an exciting route—one they hadn't considered. Soon, they were getting ready for an IPO because Darryl had assured them that was the best way for an entrepreneurial business to grow and prove its success. Emily and her family genuinely liked Darryl. Not only was he knowledgeable, confident, and charming, but also, he soon became a trusted ally to the family.

The new structure for the newly public company was simple. Four independent directors would sit on the board, along with three inside directors—Emily, Darryl, and her mother. Darryl was more than happy to handle the public-facing roles and Emily would run the business as CEO. Completely simple ... until it wasn't.

New to the rules of public companies, and with Darryl's knowledge, the family bought the assets of a bankrupt company without the approval of the independent board directors. And when the board learned about it, they were furious. Even though Darryl had been informed before the sale, he did not admit this to the board, and joined them in castigating Emily.

After that episode, Emily was met with more and more rancor with every meeting of the board of directors. The independent directors questioned her agendas with a nasty tone. They delayed decisions and looked to Darryl for advice and clarification. He, of course, was happy to oblige, and while he didn't publicly undermine Emily, she felt something was going on. She even overheard Darryl criticizing her to employees. That's when she felt a little alarm go off. She started to notice the red flags flying, and asked Darryl to explain exactly what was going on. He responded that nothing was wrong and she was being overly sensitive.

So, she was shocked when the board told her they'd called in a consulting firm to evaluate her performance. Naturally, they framed their intentions as the best interests of the company to understand "what it will take for the business to move forward."

Despite this shattering development, she met with the lead consultant and introduced him to the company's customers in person. She carefully took him through every aspect of the company, detailing its history and performance. Emily was professional and methodical during the entire process, hiding how demeaned and angry she felt.

When the report was ready, the board called an executive session of all independent board members to meet with the consultants. After an hour passed, they invited Darryl into the meeting, but not Emily. Darryl's smile was smug as he entered the meeting, while Emily waited, anxious and impatient, in her office.

The results of the report were astonishing to the board. The consultancy determined Darryl's behavior was disruptive and duplicitous. He was guilty of feeding the board obvious misinformation (translation: lies and omissions). Emily, they found, was not just a competent CEO, but also a strong one, fully connected to the business and her customers. The board had fully expected a negative report on Emily. And even though Darryl had poisoned the board with distortions and personal attacks on Emily's behavior as CEO, after the consultant's report, not one board member questioned the consultants' recommendations.

Darryl was immediately fired. The family then decided to buy back *the company and take it private. The independent board members resigned en masse.*

Emily picked up the pieces, remained CEO, and now has a strong board that she respects, and that respects her. Business is running smoothly and the company is enjoying successful growth.

In the face of betrayal of her trust by her business advisor, Emily clearly demonstrated resilience. She has a great ability to be objective in her hindsight, identifying a number of personal mistakes, from avoiding a confrontation with Darryl to being intimidated by the egos and expertise of the independent board members. At the center of Emily's resilience was her determination to protect her family's hard-earned and hard-won success. If she weakened in the face of adversity, all that her family had built would have been lost. Emily also credits her parents with her tough inner resolve. She notes that she was an "Air Force kid," and constantly moving from base to base was very difficult and disruptive. Her mother taught her that to survive, saying, "it does not matter what happens; you just move on with your life."

She also offers some lessons from her experience. She sees now that there were many red flags she ignored. The first being that you should never go public with a business without a full understanding of what is necessary, or without having complete faith in, and support of, your board. She believes now that independent outside advisors are key, because they can provide an objective reality check to the business challenges. She freely admits that she, like many women, refrained from asking too many questions or seeking advice because she did not want to appear "weak." Emily emphasizes, "Resist that temptation. If it matters, you should be able to ask enough questions to ensure you understand the issue and the implications." And finally, as both Nancy and Priscilla found, Emily believes that the minute you feel demeaned or that you are losing your identity as a strong person, trust the feeling and take action. It will never get better. It will only get worse.

Andrew's story also demonstrates the power of bouncing high after a fall.

OFF THE A-TEAM AND INTO THE COLD

Andrew left the boardroom, thrilled for his dear friend and colleague, Leda, who had just been named CEO of their well-known consumer-goods company.

As Andrew rushed into Leda's office, he smiled broadly and congratulated Leda on her phenomenal run-up to this moment.

"Well done and well-deserved. I am so happy for you."

"Thank you, Andrew. And I hope you know I need a trusted ally like you now more than ever."

Andrew moved away quickly to let the other well-wishers heap praise on Leda.

Walking through the halls, Andrew thought warmly of his ten years at the company. In addition to his personal success, he enjoyed the challenging work, as well as the relationships he had forged.

In fact, Leda and her husband, Charlie, had become close to Andrew and his partner, Stan. They often booked ski vacations and cruises together, in addition to discovering and enjoying new restaurants.

Within the next few weeks, Leda met with Andrew to ask him to join her executive leadership team.

"Andrew, I know you thrive on running your own profit and loss division with your own team, but I'm putting together a core strategy team to help me execute my corporate vision. We'll deal with issues from

thirty thousand feet to position this company for a strong future. There's a lot to do."

Leda's certainty that Andrew was the right person to be part of this daunting task was not only a compliment, but also a validation of the success he had created over the years.

Of course Andrew would sign up for this position, even though his new role was unclear. In the beginning, Andrew relished his inclusion at the center of power. Everyone in the office was aware of Andrew and Leda's close professional bond.

But it was even more exhilarating to be part of this new team, even if some of the other members had teased Leda and Andrew about their long-standing friendship and the fact that they were often able to complete each other's sentences.

"Some people," Leda reminded him. "Will say anything to knock you off your game."

Andrew's choice to follow Leda truly paid off when he was given a seat on the board of directors. It was a remarkable moment in his career. He'd never anticipated becoming an internal board member.

What happened next threw Leda and the company's finances into crisis. After Leda accepted the resignation for retirement of her CFO, she quickly discovered that the numbers did not add up. There appeared to be significant malfeasance.

Every moment of Leda's day was now consumed with understanding and rectifying this shocking development.

Days went by, and Andrew heard little from Leda even though, of course, the board was involved in resolving these critical issues. It's a temporary shift in focus, *Andrew thought.* Given the enormity of the company's financial troubles, and the need to ensure that the internal board members were not involved in any way in the financial cover-up.

Despite the logic of his exclusion, Andrew was still troubled by a continuing lack of communication and his own lack of involvement in helping solve this crisis. While Andrew wasn't completely pushed aside, he realized that information was being compartmentalized and there wasn't full transparency. It was a perplexing situation. In the past, despite the nature of the crisis, Leda would use Andrew as a sounding board to help her think through issues and to test her assumptions. This wasn't happening, and, in fact, it felt like Leda was avoiding him.

Weeks later, given the plummeting financials, a painful corporate downsizing occurred to stabilize the company. Andrew understood the necessity, but it was hard to see what was happening to the people and place he had poured so much time and energy into. Worse, because he was now part of Leda's executive team and a member of the board, everyone looked to him for answers and reassurances, but he was unable to provide them.

During this period, Andrew received many calls from headhunters expressing their interest in his skills, but he demurred. His loyalty to Leda remained, even though by then, the social side of their friendship had completely frayed. Dinners were abandoned, and vacation plans became a faded memory.

When Andrew confronted Leda about his waning role in the company, it was met with the attitude of "Can't you see I'm too busy for this? We have a company to fix. I can't deal with drama." Leda was clear that outsiders now made up her inner circle, and friendship and loyalty no longer had a seat at the table. With this, Andrew recognized that the doors had been firmly shut, and his CEO had betrayed his trust.

In the next round of corporate layoffs, without warning, Andrew's name was on the list. He agreed to take a severance package in order to find an opportunity to create a new future in a new company. Showing his strength in the face of betrayal, Andrew was able to have Leda agree to orchestrate his departure in a face-saving way, even sending out a highly complimentary email to the organization.

For Andrew, resilience gave him the confidence to move forward, knowing he had done nothing wrong.

In his words, "I decided to let go of the bitterness I felt toward the CEO and her henchmen because it wasn't healthy or productive. I do mourn the loss of a once-deep friendship. The minute I left, the universe sent me numerous interesting, lucrative, and fun opportunities to work with great people on issues I care about, where I can add value and be appreciated. It's a good feeling." Andrew has thus joined the society of "high bouncers!"

John Mark Haney and Leslie Hardie, therapists and authors of "Psychotherapeutic Considerations for Working With Betrayed Spouses," have mapped out an intriguing "recovery curve that can readily apply to all betrayal recoveries."[33] It works like this:

First, is *realization*. The simple act of packing away denial and confronting the event. It's getting past the "I was stupid to be so trusting. Crazy not to see what was in front of me. I'm so embarrassed. What now?" Accepting reality sounds easy, but depending on the depth of the feelings of the betrayed, the timeline for acceptance can be weeks, months, or stretch even longer, to years.

Second, is *reaction*. As the impact of betrayal sinks in, a grieving process begins for all that was lost. "I'll never be creative director, president, confidant, whatever ... again." And it's charged with emotions—anger, fear, guilt, loneliness, and shame. This tsunami of feelings and constant replaying of the betrayal must de-escalate to a more normal state to get to the next stage.

Third, is *release*. It's like taking a deep, purifying breath. The past can't be revised or reinvented, so let it go. Decide on a forward-going path and commit to it. Promise yourself there will be no more

---

33 Hardie, "Psychotherapeutic Considerations for Working With Betrayed Spouses."

exhausting, middle-of-the-night rehashes and recriminations. "If only" must be seen as a fantasy; that ship has sailed.

Last, is *recommitment*. This is the best part. While you can't erase the betrayal from your life, it's important to recognize it and learn from it. Personal growth is the singular benefit amid the chaos. While the betrayal will always have meaning, it no longer has the power to define you or diminish you.

As our survivors, Nancy, Phyllis, Emily, and Andrew all learned, resilience, that ability to bounce back even higher than before, is the key to recovery. That ability to be objective about what happened, where they could think and talk about the betrayer without the heat of intense emotion. Only then was it possible to absolve themselves of blame, understand the needs and goals of the betrayer, and to gain insight into the motivation that resulted in the betrayal. Through reflection, distance, self-confidence, and self-knowledge, these survivors moved on. They each knew when they were "over it," and when it was time to shape their brand-new future. They truly learned how to "bounce."

Following is a checklist for moving on:

1. Mourn your loss.

2. Eliminate any and all "what if" scenarios.

3. Be nice to yourself.

4. Celebrate your survival.

5. Realize that you are trustworthy.

6. Make a list of all your strengths.

7. Own the betrayal, but close off the humiliation (enough!).

8. Write down everything that happened. Wait twenty-four hours and read it as an objective observer. Burn the paper.

9. Talk to supportive people. Do not hide behind a curtain of shame.

10. Be mindful about how you tell your story. Start sentences with "I wish I" not "I failed."

11. Note to self: forgiveness isn't required; it's your choice alone.

12. Find people you can trust and keep them close.

13. Imagine your new future. Make it real.

14. Trust (but verify) someone new.

15. Celebrate your future.

A word about rebuilding trust. A betrayal can tend to make you hyper-vigilant about every aspect of a relationship, and that's an exhausting strategy for living life. It can also lead to isolation for the fear that "something could happen again." While it might, it will certainly be different, so take heart that you have learned from your experience and can apply it to many new situations.

As Jenny Sanford shared in the *New York Times* account of her remarriage in 2018, "If trust requires a confident relationship with the unknown ... You ask yourself, 'Can I love again?' But the better question is, 'What happens if I get hurt again?' At the end of the day, you have to be willing to take the risk."

And when you begin to trust again, remember to trust wisely.

TAKEAWAYS

1. Resilience is the springboard to a better life.

2. Let your recovery happen at its own pace. Listen to your own body and mind. You'll be over it when you're over it.

3. Stay clear on your identity and your self-worth. Don't overlook your achievements in the face of all the flying emotional debris. Remember your core strengths—no matter how long ago it was that you used them—and maximize them.

4. Yes, there are people who will betray you, but, if you reach out, there are more people who will support and honor you. Find them and keep them close.

CHAPTER EIGHT

Betrayal–Lessons from the War Zone

There's a reason that the windshield is bigger than the rearview mirrors.

*I never thought I would be seventy and single, but it's
a far better state than seventy and miserable.*

*The minute you settle for less than you deserve,
you get even less than you settled for.*
—Maureen Dowd

The above quotes—the first two, by survivors—typify the lessons from our interviews and research.

Our final collection of stories brings together insights, observations, and experiences from previous chapters to highlight the lessons of experience. These are lessons that exemplify the strong survival instincts and resilience that helped people dig themselves out of the black hole of betrayal, and get themselves onto a path to a better place, armed with confidence, hope, and anticipation.

Imagine it's a cloudless day and you're hiking on a woodland trail that you have hiked on for many years. Suddenly, without warning, the earth around you crumbles, the ground collapses beneath your feet, and you fall into an abyss. That is what the experience of betrayal feels like—everything you thought you knew has suddenly and irrevocably given way beneath your feet.

As we have learned, betrayal is far more than a bump in the road. It is an all-consuming echo chamber of deceit and lies. But, as we have also learned, the moment of betrayal can also become the moment of liberation from a stressful past and the door to a new and exciting future.

That is exactly what is Bridget discovered when her husband's death uncovered twenty years of deception.

THE RAINBOW'S END

"Don't even think of paying those credit card bills," her accountant warned. "It could make you liable for all the other debts he incurred before he died."

Bridget was no stranger to widowhood. Twenty years ago, her first husband died, leaving her with two small boys. At the time, she was devoted to her children and her burgeoning career. It was enough to get her through the initial pain of loss, but inside, she knew she didn't want to be alone forever.

That was when her good friend, Kitty, stepped in.

"There's someone Ted and I can't wait for you to meet," she said.

"Really, Kitty, a blind date?" Bridget demurred.

"Think of it as a little push in the right direction," Kitty urged. "He's smart, fun, and comes from a very, very rich family, the kind they breed in Texas."

It turned out to be a great and lively date. Bob was very attractive, bright, and made Bridget laugh. As they became a couple, she noticed he wasn't shy about touting his family's holdings and wealth. More than once, he told her his family owned a sports team and racetrack.

Bob soon made it known to Bridget that he had twenty million in inherited gold tucked safely in a Swiss deposit box. Unfortunately, it was being held in litigation due to proof of ownership issues. Yes, there was a whiff of arrogance in all this, but Bridget was ridiculously smitten.

For three years they dated, traveled, and enjoyed their life together, as a couple, and also with her sons. It was a situation Bridget soon wanted to make permanent. They had spoken of marriage, but if she was honest, Bridget would have to admit that she had kept the pressure on because she wanted a father for her two sons, Tom and Brian. He was fully engaged with her boys and they responded with affection. So engaged, in fact, that he spent far more time with them than with the sons from his first marriage. He explained this as a heartbreak for him, but he'd had no choice. His wife was angry and vicious. She had poisoned the children's relationship with him with lies about him.

The afternoon that Bob presented her with his grandmother's engagement ring, Bridget was overcome with happiness. Life was complete with this marvelous man, her successful career, and her sons. She had absolutely no misgivings, not a one.

Days before their wedding, Bob told Bridget that he was having a cash flow issue.

"Nothing serious, darling," he smiled. "I just need to borrow a small amount. I promise to repay the money in a flash."

Bridget pulled out her purse and handed him a check for $150,000. Ever the gentleman, Bob wrote her an IOU with a flourish. She smiled and popped the note into her desk drawer. It would soon be time to say their vows.

Once married, they traveled extensively and enjoyed tennis tournaments and the simple pleasures of being a family. From the beginning, Bob asked Bridget to assume responsibility for their expenses. After all, he was paying child support and alimony to his first wife, and all would be fine as soon as the "messy" legal issues over the Swiss bank account were settled. This was fine with Bridget, as she truly believed that it was just a matter of time before Bob took on financial responsibility for her and her sons.

"Bridge, I've got a sensational idea for an online business," Bob excitedly told her. "Photographic prints, the finest quality. Portraits of celebrities, rock stars, world leaders. It'll keep me occupied and bring in some money while you're toiling away in that corporate world of yours." Bridget agreed, it would be a good, shall we say ... hobby, and any extra cash would be very appreciated. Of course, the start-up funds would come out of her wallet, but this was just another way of helping Bob keep busy till the thorny legal issues in Switzerland were settled.

Bridget had adapted to Bob's seemingly endless financial problems, and for that reason, she continued, throughout their marriage, to file her taxes separately. And since there were no joint accounts, she felt insulated from any expensive surprises regarding his debt.

Twenty years passed. The marriage was a comfortable and happy one, once Bridget completely ignored Bob's ongoing promise of the pot of gold. But in the back of her mind she always thought, What if it is true?

The onset of Bob's terminal illness stunned both of them. And the boys, now young men, were genuinely upset. The shock woke Bridget up to the fact that Switzerland was never going to happen. But Bob kept feeding the delusion, telling her to expect someone from Europe to untangle the mess. Bridget did know that she and the boys were the recipients of his significant life-insurance policy, as she and Bob had met with their broker to designate his beneficiaries. Bob also promised to leave Bridget's sons everything from his parents' trust, and, of course, the magical Swiss bank account funds would go to her. Bridget, trusting him, as always, believed every word.

But what about his increasing gambling debts? As Bob lay dying, Bridget saw strange charges on her American Express account. It turned out that Bob was filling his waning days with online gambling. While he promised to stop, Bridget, ever caring, did not have the heart to freeze her credit card. The daily debt level increased exponentially throughout his illness.

The betrayal of her trust only became apparent after Bob's death. In the end, Bridget owed $250,000 to Visa and American Express. It was a ridiculous sum. She was stunned by her husband's reckless behavior, and angry at herself for having no idea that this was occurring at that level.

Bridget hired an investigator to check on the Swiss account. When the investigator found there was no Swiss account—that it was all a myth—she wasn't totally surprised, because she'd expected as much. Then, Bridget learned from their insurance broker that the beneficiaries of his policy had been changed from her sons to his children from his first marriage. Somehow, Bob had neglected to tell her that he met separately with their insurance broker and told him to make the change, which he promised Bridget had agreed to. His parents' trust was also earmarked for his children, as the requirement was that the recipients be blood relatives—a small fact that he had obviously "forgotten" to mention.

The only funds available to Bridget were the Social Security survivor benefits, and, since he had not worked in over twenty years, it was minimal. After a reasonable time for mourning, their many friends who had lent Bob significant amounts of money over the years came forward with his famous IOUs.

And the final betrayal? His grandmother's heirloom engagement ring was cubic zirconia simply dating back to the 1980s.

Bridget could no longer deny the cold reality that Bob had knowingly and intentionally lied to her for over twenty years, continuing his deceits until the day he died.

Asked what it took to survive Bob's multiple betrayals of her trust, Bridget is reflective and pragmatic. Yes, Bob duped her into supporting him for twenty years. And, yes, there were many red flags that she chose to ignore. But, incredibly, she also admits that her marriage to Bob brought her great joy far beyond an escape from her loneliness as a young widow. As for her two boys? He was a wonderful and loving father.

In Bridget's own words: "Try to understand that Bob was the first person to make me laugh again after I was widowed. There is an old Russian proverb that says, 'Better to be slapped with the truth than kissed with a lie,' so the question that raises is, would I still pay close to a million dollars to be married to a man who made me and my sons happy for so long, even knowing what happened? I still haven't answered that."

Bridget experienced the negative outcomes of blind trust, but the counterpoint was the joy and contentment she found in her marriage to Bob.

Another important part of Bridget's ability to survive his betrayal was her financial self-sufficiency. As a very senior corporate executive, and director on many boards, her salary was more than sufficient to support the family. And, despite her trust in Bob, she also heeded the red flags.

This is the arena in which she practiced wise trust and prepared for the worst-case scenario. As she explains, "Yes, there was financial disappointment, but not financial ruin, because I protected my money and my income. Once you have misgivings, listen to your gut and lock everything down. Always insist on a prenup for a second marriage, and ensure that you have no joint accounts. Wills and beneficiaries can be changed. Trust no one but yourself."

For Bridget, the worst part of the betrayal was her postmortem realization that she could never believe that anything he'd ever said was true. "That realization impacted my confidence in my own judgment. I felt so stupid that I had not seen any of this—especially when I had to tell my sons. They loved him." Revenge wasn't possible; he was dead. Bridget has never fully forgiven him, as his betrayal was intentional from the beginning.

But she decided to tap into the store of resilience that had served her well when her first husband died, keep marching, and get on with life. "I stopped feeling like a victim and stopped defending him. Luckily, his debts were not my debts, and if our friends couldn't understand that, then I did not need them. I would find new friends. And I did."

Bridget's strength was both philosophical and pragmatic—a potent combination to help anyone climbing out of the abyss of betrayal.

Karen's story of betrayal is also about a second marriage. Only this time, the betrayer is her stepdaughter.

J'ACCUSE

Karen was on the gilded path to a happy marriage. She and Bret were in love and ready to build a life together. Bret had been divorced for eight years and had a teenage daughter, Angie. Both Karen and Angie liked spending time together and got on well. Karen even got along with Bret's former wife, as the divorce had been easy and amicable.

But like any child of divorce who moved between two households, Angie was a master at pushing the guilt button. Bret forgave a lot of her behavior, because he believed she was still dealing with the disappointment of her parent's split, and he felt that he owed her unconditional love.

Yet sometimes, Angie would look for situations to force Bret to choose between her wishes and Karen's.

"Dad, please help me tell Karen we aren't going to spend the day at a stupid museum. Let's change her mind and do something fun!" was a typical refrain.

Karen's good nature and Bret's sense of fairness got them through a lot of Angie's teenage dramas. And it seemed this new family unit was on a solid path forward.

Shortly after they were married, Angie asked for a car of her own.

"I'm sixteen, guys, and it's, like, really important that I have my own wheels," she informed them at the dinner table. "Mom said no, but I know that my daddy and my good friend Karen understand me so much better than Mom. And Karen would never want to be the evil stepmother, would you, Karen? So, I just know that you guys will say yes."

Bret and Karen told her they'd discuss it. Both agreed Angie was too immature for the responsibility of owning a car, so they offered up an alternate idea: Bret and Karen would chauffeur Angie anywhere, anytime she wanted to go, plus give her an unlimited Uber allowance until graduation. It seemed like a win-win for all parties.

"I don't want that," Angie said with her face getting redder by the minute. "I want my car. I deserve it for all the crap you have put me through." Catching her breath, Angie continued to rant at her father.

"And if you don't, I swear I'll go to the police and tell them you're a child molester, and that's why my mother divorced you!"

Horrified by her reaction, Bret stood even firmer and did not give into Angie's demands and ridiculous threat. He could not believe that his own child could be that vicious and vindictive.

Unfortunately, the threat became reality.

Days later, Social Services and the police came to the door, acting on Angie's complaint.

It took many interviews, investigations, and hefty legal fees, but Bret was finally cleared from his daughter's false allegations. However, Angie's betrayal would never be forgotten by Bret or Karen.

Karen was filled with anger, and was heartbroken over the toll this false accusation had on Bret and his reputation. It took her over a year to get her emotions under control. Ultimately, after court-mandated therapy, Angie apologized and asked for forgiveness. In time, Bret forgave his daughter, because she was, after all, his daughter. But his forgiveness came at a price. He refused to pay anything for her "lifestyle," with the exception of health care, and ultimately, college.

Karen had far more trouble with the idea of forgiveness, and has not been able to find her way there. Instead, she moves between anger and ambivalence. Knowing that Angie would always be part of her future, Karen decided it was best to support Bret and give him a wide berth on anything involving Angie.

In retrospect, Angie never thought through the consequences of her plan to win a car. She had no idea what the full force of the report would bring down on her father. Naïvely, she believed that once her father agreed to a car, she'd tell Social Services and the police it was just an innocent game. Little did Angie know that nothing is that easy when it comes to a report of parental abuse. She never anticipated the colossal problems she'd face trying to recant her accusation. And what it would cost her father in legal fees and investigations to clear his name and expunge his record—not to mention the emotional distress.

Many women who enter a second or third marriage will face a variety of family issues. They're part of the landscape, and need to be dealt with head-on if the marriage is to succeed. That's lesson one. Lesson two is to adopt the stance of strategic patience. Karen did, and while she supported Brett, she knew Angie was *his* issue. Seeking revenge or granting forgiveness was not Karen's right or role.

The mutual respect Karen and Bret had for one another led them through this difficult time. She didn't pressure Bret to reject his daughter, and Bret didn't push Karen to embrace her. Neither one wanted this to be a permanent issue impacting their marriage. So they gave each other the right to determine their own timetable for recovery, and supported each other on their chosen path.

Betrayals, small and large, can happen in every family (granted, this one was especially destructive). Karen realized she had to think of the long game. She knew Angie would be at family events, and spending time in their home, so they had to open a line of communication and rebuild trust in each other. They learned, as Eleanor Roosevelt observed, that "you gain strength, courage, and confidence by every experience in which you really stop to look fear in the face ... You must do the thing you think you cannot do." For Karen and Bret, they learned that they could never go back to the place they once were, but at least they could move forward, together.

Even more soul shattering is Jessica's story, whose lessons help move us further along in our search for tools for survival.

As you will see, Jessica exemplifies Robert Louis Stevenson's quote, "Life is not a matter of holding good cards, but of playing a poor hand well."

MY BOYFRIEND'S BACK

"Anyone home?" yelled Jessica, after returning from a full day of high school and soccer practice. At first, she didn't hear anyone, but then

realized that there were sounds coming from her mother's room. Worried that something was wrong, Jessica ran to the room and flung open the door. And then she stopped in shock and horror. In her mother's bed was her mother and Jessica's boyfriend, Sam.

It was a blinding version of The Graduate, *minus Dustin Hoffman and Anne Bancroft. As Jessica ran down the stairs, she felt her stomach drop and her eyes fill with tears.*

This wasn't some random high school girl who had stolen Sam; it was her own mother. Her thirty-eight-year-old mother. Her world had just ended.

Processing this incredible betrayal of everything she held true and dear, Jessica bolted into her room and tried to stop thinking about killing both of them. Steeling herself, she ran through an objective review of Sam's recent behavior. He was a musician, and since graduating from high school, he'd made Jessica's home his own when he wasn't on tour. She noticed he'd been around her house more and more, but attributed it to his love for her. Obviously, this was not the case.

There was a soft knock on the door and her mother appeared.

"Jess, I know this is uncomfortable for you," she began. "But the relationship Sam and I have is an adult one, nothing like your seventeen-year-old crush."

The words simply fanned Jessica's anger. But there was more to come.

"Once you understand how serious we are about our love, you'll know why I'm asking your father for a divorce," her mother continued. "Sam and I want to live together openly. Since you have such a great relationship with Sam, this transition should be easy for you. It's your senior year. We can all live together until you leave for college."

Openly? *Jessica thought.* You lived a lie in front of me, but want to be noble enough to tell my father that you have betrayed us all?

Jessica's father, Paolo, was living and working in Argentina, and

Jessica was sure he would be as devastated as she was by her mother's news—probably even more.

After a week, Jessica came up with a plan. She would move to Buenos Aires to live with her father. They could support each other emotionally, and it would prevent Jessica from seeing Sam and her mother together every day. Sam, of course, said nothing to Jessica, casually assuming everything was cool.

Jessica found it strange that her father didn't answer her urgent texts or calls. It was as if he'd disappeared from life. She felt like an orphan.

When she finally reached Paolo, she eagerly told him of her plans.

"Jessica, if you come down here, every time I look at you, I'll be reminded of your mother's infidelity," he said. "I can't cope."

By this point, she certainly didn't know who was the adult in the family—or if she was the only one. Suddenly she was faced with her mother living with Jessica's ex-boyfriend, and her father, who was paralyzed with depression.

With nowhere to run, Jessica pushed her fury out of the way and focused on her studies and love of sports. She had one year before high school graduation, and then it was off to college and out of her prison.

Every day, she found strength in knowing this wouldn't last forever. The Churchill quote, "If you're going through hell, keep going," became her mantra. She knew that in order to survive, she had to find something no one could take away from her.

That turned out to be soccer. Her coach inspired the team by encouraging each player to separate short-term goals from long-term ones. By achieving success in the short term, they were setting the stage for the long term.

Immediately, Jessica saw that parallel in her life. She began to focus on dealing with the day-to-day dual trauma of living in the house with her mother and Sam, and her father's physical and emotional distance. She focused solely on her short-term goal of getting good grades and being part of a winning soccer team. Then she worked on her long-term goal of getting into the college of her choice—far from home—and inventing and living a life on her own terms.

With the help of her therapist, she learned about the stages of resilience, and realized she had to withdraw from the serious emotional chaos that was a constant reminder of her betrayal.

It worked.

With her therapist's help, Jessica understood her father's need to withdraw before recovering and moving on from her mother's betrayal of his trust and love. Over time, Jessica reconciled with her father, and forgave him for being weak when she needed him to be strong. Today, she has a close relationship with him. That helped her to begin to trust in love again. Jessica is now married and has a young son. Her father is a regular guest in her home, but her mother will never be welcome.

She remains estranged from the woman who betrayed her, the woman she calls Mrs. Robinson. As she learned from her therapist, "Families are like a tree; sometimes you need to cut off the diseased branches or they will kill the tree." To Jessica, her mother will always be a diseased branch.

Why could Jessica forgive her father and not her mother? Jessica saw her mother's betrayal as a crisis of character. Her mother had put self-interest above the interests of her husband and daughter, and was completely incapable of understanding the damage that she'd wrought by seducing her daughter's boyfriend. What kind of mother does that?

Her father, however, was different. He was in so much pain that he couldn't think beyond his own needs in the face of his traumatic response to his wife's betrayal, and as a result, could not even begin to understand the impact on his daughter. And that makes it a crisis of judgment.

Forgiveness may be possible in a crisis of judgment, but, our survivors have told us, it is much more difficult, if not impossible, in a crisis of character. Matt's betrayal provides another perspective on a crisis of character.

WHAT YOU DON'T KNOW CAN HURT YOU

Quite simply, Matt's betrayal shook the halls of academe. He was savaged by the most severe case of fraud ever perpetrated by an "esteemed Doctor of Genetics," Dr. Theodore Caffey. Right under his nose, directly under the auspices of the university, Dr. Caffey had fudged results with one hand, and grabbed money from Matt's investors with the other. Sheer genius put to shady use.

Before Matt had chosen Dr. Caffey as the designated head of genetic research, he studied the man's resume and history. Dr. Caffey was the golden boy. He'd attended Harvard on scholarship, then Cambridge. He'd been published in more top academic and medical journals than any of his peers. Next, he'd landed at the National Institute of Health, and while there, started an outside enterprise, which he'd sold to a European company for a fantastic profit.

Dr. Caffey was energetic, always in the lab, and always ready to hold forth at medical symposiums. He was summa cum everything.

Even his personal life was golden. Married to a world-famous surgeon, Dr. Caffey was always looking to enhance his five-star credentials.

Based on these credentials, a group of people, including Matt, were willing to invest in Dr. Caffey to create groundbreaking research at the university. His role was clear. Dr. Caffey would define the research agenda—focusing on innovative new treatments, lead the experiments, deliver confirmation of their efficacy, and assist in monetizing the results.

The university agreed to the role of sponsor and oversight. Matt and his investors would put up the requisite money to support the lab for this work.

What could possibly go wrong?

Initially, Matt urged the doctor to take advantage of an advisory board of experts to provide ongoing input and to serve as a sounding board for the direction of his work.

Dr. Caffey bristled, "Please, Matt, leave these so-called experts out of this. All they'll do is steal my work."

"Don't be so hasty, an advisory board could help," Matt responded.

"Do you want a board or me?" Dr. Caffey pushed back. "I'll give you the results. Now let's leave things as they are."

The exchange left Matt uncomfortable, and yet he did nothing to ease his concerns. Instead he decided to trust Dr. Caffey and leave well enough alone. After all, Dr. Caffey was the genius, right?

Matt also questioned why one of their top research associates had walked out. It made no sense, as it seemed liked the ideal situation in which to make a name for oneself. Although he asked the associate, no real explanation was given, other than quality of life and needing more leisure time. He tried to extract more answers, but none were forthcoming, so once again, he let it go.

Dr. Caffey's total control over his lab continued. It became the sole prerequisite for his retention. But after many unfilled requests for material updates, Matt's increasing frustration finally led him to hire another research scientist and a forensic auditor to conduct a full investigation.

Reviewing the records, it was clear that Dr. Caffey's research was a fabrication. No studies had been completed. The lab was in chaos. He had been funneling the invested research funds into multiple bank accounts all along to enable his outsized lifestyle. Coupled with this astounding revelation was the fact that the university had not noticed the steady stream of disappearing funds.

Ultimately, Matt and the university settled the accounts, each recognizing the other's culpability in enabling Dr. Caffey's duplicity by ignoring the red flags. The reputational and financial cost to Matt, however, was significant.

Matt provides us with an outstanding lesson on the dual dangers of over-reliance on blind trust, coupled with a refusal to see the red flags waving on the horizon. As Matt told us, no one in his position should ever be as naïve and trusting as he was with Dr. Caffey.

With the gift of hindsight, he realized that there were six separate events over a five-year period that were major red-flag events. But what did he do? He asked Dr. Caffey for explanations and accepted them at face value. Despite the red flags, he never called in outside experts to judge Dr. Caffey's processes or work until it was too late. Instead, he was overly respectful of Dr. Caffey's desire for independence and secrecy. All the clues were there, but, despite his concerns, he chose to remain blind and clueless, and he clearly paid a very expensive price. As he says, if he were given an opportunity for a "do-over," even if he were to choose Dr. Caffey, he would insist on transparency.

He also would act on every red flag through constant requirements for updates, have an advisory board, and never believe anything that isn't made clear through demonstration. He would never again blindly trust someone, no matter how many times he is told "Trust me."

Our next story is about Hallie, who suffered three betrayals, yet kept her external focus on moving forward through each one. She has many lessons for us to consider.

TWICE BURNED, THREE TIMES SHY

Hallie is very familiar with the following quote by Robert Frost: "Home is the place where, when you have to go there, they have to take you in."

Hallie was married, pregnant with her first child, and—after a tough climb—a vice president at a real estate investment firm. She was "livin' large," as they say, until the day her husband came home and said, "Hallie, I know we will always love each other, and because of that, I know you want me to be happy. I have found my soul mate, and I want a divorce. Of course, I will always be there for you and our child, but differently."

Reeling from that shock, she was still processing how she would manage as a soon-to-be single mom and an executive in a demanding role. But there was more to come.

A few days later, her CEO called her into his office, and said, "Hallie, as you know, we have been looking for strategic alternatives for our company. We have decided to split it up and sell to two different buyers. Your job is redundant for both of them, so we will be giving you a great severance package and any support you need in finding your next job. But think of the bright side—you'll have an opportunity to stay home and bond with your new baby."

Grieving for her two losses, and desperate for the comfort of people who loved her unconditionally, Hallie and her newborn son went back to Hallie's parents' home in Iowa. Overwhelmed, Hallie considered staying there, as her mother suggested. But then her father, always her best cheerleader, said, "There are no failures in life, just detours you didn't expect."

With that advice, Hallie realized that her time of personal retreat and self-care was over, and that she had built up the necessary inner strength to move forward and create a new future in the industry in which she had already made a mark. She gathered her child and her self-confidence and returned to California. There, she began calling her contacts, saying, "I'm back!" Much to her delight, she found a new opportunity and sources of joy.

Fast-forward twenty years. Hallie had become extremely successful. She was married and had two sons: Dan, from her brief first marriage, and Will, from her second. Once again, she experienced a defining moment of betrayal.

Hallie looked directly at her eldest son, Dan, and her younger son, Will, barely able to conceal her fury.

"So you're telling me you have known for over a year that your dad was having an affair, and you both decided to keep it from me?" she asked, incredulously.

"Mom, we were protecting you, and that's why we weren't around too much. We didn't think we could keep the secret if you asked us directly," Will explained.

"And why exactly?" Hallie demanded. "Did I need protection? Since when have I ever been a fragile flower? Did fragility truly describe me as a mother and an executive as you were growing up?"

"Well, Dad said that you couldn't handle it, and he's your husband; he knows you better than we do. Maybe you pretended to be strong for us, but he knew the real you," Dan responded timidly.

"You weren't protecting me; you were protecting your father. He totally conned you to help him hide his affair from me. How does that feel?" Hallie said with great disdain and despair.

Granted, Hallie's marriage had been troubled for some time, but this turn of events led her to make a firm decision. She asked her husband to leave the house immediately.

Hallie couldn't believe her husband had burdened the boys with his lies and deceit. She was furious with her sons, but could forgive their betrayal because they had been misled by tales of Hallie's imaginary depression and alleged inability to cope with life.

Having been betrayed in the past, Hallie knew that the best next step was self-protection and compassion. She needed to regroup and find her old self. If her children thought that she was weak and needed protection, maybe she was giving off the wrong vibe. And there was no better place to regroup than Paris, where she could lose herself in the museums and Sunday markets. She bolstered her belief with the advice of a friend who, upon hearing the story of her betrayal, quoted French novelist and poet Anatole France: "To accomplish great things, we must not only act but also dream; not only plan, but also believe."

Just as her father's advice had galvanized her energy and resolve, her friend's advice had the same power. The time away was restorative. It rekindled her entrepreneurial spirit, and Hallie felt her confidence quickly return. Her ability to bounce back came bouncing back.

Returning home, Hallie began looking for a new business. She saw opportunity in a new model for building master plan communities. Her past career in real estate development and mixed-use planning convinced investors to provide venture funding.

The rewards followed for both Hallie and her investors. It was a good feeling to have this success following such a failure in her personal life.

As the company grew, more assets were needed to fuel its growth, and Hallie thought the time was right to sell. She chose a large and resource-rich Canadian company. She was precise in her contract with the new owners that she would be a majority voice in the process of identifying and choosing her successor.

Soon after the sale, the buyers chose a successor. Hallie had reservations, but since they knew him, she was willing to give him the opportunity to succeed before she moved on to her next venture. Jack arrived with a good deal of arrogance, but not a lot of experience in mixed-use planning. His planning credentials were not in this type of planning, but Hallie continued to work with Jack, giving him the benefit of the doubt.

As time went on, she knew he knew he was over his head and

under-qualified. Hallie didn't want to see what she had built end up in his hands. She refused to name him as her successor.

That's when the bullying began.

"Lady, lose the attitude," he'd snicker. "And start acting like the rest of us. This isn't your company anymore."

Jack insisted she change her management style.

"Loosen it up, babe," he added with a wink. Clearly, Jack wanted her gone because she could expose him.

Ignoring the agreement Hallie had in place, Jack fired her without warning.

"Clean out your office, and do it over the weekend," he demanded.

Although Jack had no legal right to break the contract, the Canadian owners refused to honor the terms, claiming that since she had initially agreed to put Jack in place, they had complied with the intent.

Hallie refused to back down.

"Honor the full agreement whereby my approval is required," she told the Canadians, "or I will sue."

Hallie sued, won the case, and received a substantial monetary judgment against the Canadian company. There was only one stipulation: she could never again enter the offices of her former business.

So karma decided to pay a quick visit to Jack. It turned out that Hallie owned the building, and her son Dan managed it. Now, Hallie enjoyed the perverse pleasure of taunting Jack by coming and going as the owner. And, of course, Dan, as the building manager, always determined how quickly tenant requests were met.

So much for the weak-kneed, depressed, fragile woman painted by her second husband. Though betrayed multiple times, Hallie came through each betrayal more competent and confidant than before. She is truly the embodiment of resilience.

At first read, it seems Hallie was a superwoman to deal so well with the betrayals of two husbands followed by a corporate betrayal. But let's look more closely at her lessons. While she used wise trust in dealing with her work life, blind trust took precedence in her love life. Blinded by love, she did not use her savvy to trust and verify in either marriage. Yet her inner strength and the support and wise advice of her father and her friend helped her tap into her inner resources to look to the future rather than dwell in the past.

It was her ability to build success in her business life that helped to bolster her ego, despite the marital betrayals. By focusing on success rather than failure, she pulled herself into the future. And she gives credit to the support of her friends and parents for being a critical component in her ability to move forward. As she notes, "They were there for me, never judged me, wouldn't let me crawl into a hole and disappear, and always loved me."

Hallie is a first-rate example of summoning one's inner strength and maintaining external focus as an important step to move on and up.

Through our interviews, we have learned that, despite the initial trauma, pain, and humiliation, most of us survive and recover from betrayal and become stronger and wiser as a direct result of the devastating experience. Recovery is not a single point in time; it is an ongoing process. And forgiveness, if it occurs, takes place only after the healing process is complete. Forgiveness is never the goal. The only goal is to move strongly and confidently into your new future. One day, you'll discover there are simply more ups than downs. Hang on to that, because it will steer you through darker moments. As Dr. Martin Luther King Jr. wisely noted, "Darkness cannot drive out darkness; only light can do that."[34] Opening a door to another dark

---

34 King, *Stride Toward Freedom*.

room gets you nowhere; you must keep opening doors until you find sunlight.

This strategy is reinforced by Dr. Tiffany Towers, a clinical and forensic psychologist who says, "If you focus your attention on getting yourself emotionally, mentally, and physically healthier, not only will you feel better, but you will be able to handle future difficulties with more grace and wisdom."[35]

The stories in this chapter were chosen because they brought together many of the insights and observations we have previously made. They also illustrate important takeaways that can serve as guideposts for planning your future, post-betrayal.

We have learned to keep in mind the gorilla video we described in Chapter Two. Most people do not see the gorilla even though it looms large. The gorilla represents the warning signs that show up before betrayal. Relying on blind trust makes you see only what you want to see. Even if you think you know someone, it's possible you really don't.

Another learning is to be proactive in preventing betrayal by relying on this incredible early warning system called your gut. Ignore it at your own peril. Misgivings can raise serious questions. Anxiety can be your best friend. Trust your gut to tell you when a red flag is flying. If something feels wrong, it probably is wrong.

We have also learned that moving forward with your life takes strength and self-compassion. Begin by not judging yourself too harshly after a betrayal. As Phyllis wisely realized after her husband's pornography addiction spiraled out of control, "I didn't do anything wrong. He did. He betrayed me and violated everything we agreed to and believed in. Why should I be made to be the guilty party?"

Another lesson for moving on is to realize that, as one of our

---

35 Cox, "Ever Wanted to Get Revenge? Try This Instead."

survivors wisely said, "You have to live through your pain to cure it." Good advice, as long as it doesn't stall your recovery.

Moving on is all about the pivot. Pivots happen all the time in successful businesses. When something unexpected or negative happens, leaders learn from it, build on that learning, and use their energy and newfound insights to move in a different and better direction. Apply that to betrayal, and you'll realize no one but you can determine your value and your path ahead. You can pivot whenever necessary to increase your chances of success.

Also, remember strategic patience. While it's tempting to fight all the injustices betrayal sets in motion, slow down. It's a lot easier to overcome one problem at a time. And, as we have seen repeatedly, sometimes they take care of themselves when karma comes calling. But it's important to realize that, like all of us, sometimes karma sleeps late.

Now, for the touchy subject of love. No doubt about it, it's always a pure leap into blind trust, which is why a betrayal in love cuts us off at the knees. Getting through the pain is mind numbing, but finding new love is possible and probable—if you want it to be. When and if you decide to start dating again, keep your "crap detector" tuned to a high frequency.

Finally, as Bridget and others learned, you can soften the potential blow of betrayal by a loved one by having prepared yourself financially even when you still have stars in your eyes. This may sound calculating, but it's smart—especially today, when second and even third marriages abound. Prenups are a necessity, and a good idea for first marriages, too. Do not give up your personal bank accounts. File taxes separately. Commingling funds and securities is asking for trouble, should something bad happen to your marriage.

One last thought from the woman who spent a lifetime giving us advice on the challenge of moving on:

> *If we could sell our experiences for what they*
> *cost us, we'd all be millionaires.*
> — **Abigail Van Buren ("Dear Abby")**

TAKEAWAYS

1. In determining your next steps, you must decide whether you want to be the horse or the rider. It's always better to be the rider.

2. Once you have misgivings, listen to your gut and lock everything down.

3. "Always insist on a prenup for a second marriage, and ensure that you have no joint accounts. Wills and beneficiaries can be changed. Trust no one but yourself."

4. If it's not your fight, it is not your right or role to seek revenge or grant forgiveness.

5. "If you're going through hell, keep going" (Winston Churchill).

6. Never blindly trust anyone who rejects appropriate oversight and says simply, "Trust me."

Epilogue

Life always offers you a second chance. It's called tomorrow.
—Dylan Thomas, Poet

People always ask, "What is the most important lesson you have learned from these survivors?"

Actually, there's a three-part answer to the question.

Part one is "Listen to your gut," because it is an incredible natural warning system. We learned it can help you sense a betrayal before it becomes a reality. Instead of closing your eyes or creating excuses for someone else's odd behavior, listen carefully to your uneasy feelings. Those nagging doubts can help you avoid a betrayal, or at the very least, lessen the impact of one.

As Kelly McGonigal notes in her TED Talk, it is important to make stress your friend, for stress creates the biology of courage, and when you reach out to others, you create the environment for your resilience to take hold.[36]

---

36 McGonigal, "How to Make Stress Your Friend."

Her message is to redefine anxiety. Don't bury your head when the nerves first hit. Think of them as a terrific wake-up call, and use them to your advantage.

Part two is "Hold on to your power." Before you read our book, you probably thought to yourself, *what kind of power does a betrayed person have?* We hope that the stories of our survivors have shown you that even while you are navigating through a fog of deception and hurt, you do hold some cards; you just need to step back and see them. They can become a platform for a better future. So don't give your personal power away. Here's an example: you—and you alone—decide whether or not to forgive a betrayer. Don't think of forgiveness as giving your betrayer a "get out of jail free card." By recognizing and addressing the new challenges, making decisions about your next steps, and retaining your sense of self, you reclaim your power.

Most importantly, holding on to your personal power gives you control over your current and future path so you don't feel like flotsam and jetsam, carried away by the tide of betrayal. Those who recover best never relinquish their power to the betrayer.

Part three is "Have the courage to move forward." And this involves letting go. Facing the fact that you aren't in control of certain events is important because you can never create the perfect do-over to fix everything. To begin the act of recovery, look the nasty circumstances in the eye and see them for what they are. The fallout from betrayal says more about the betrayer's values than it does about you, so toss the bad stuff in the garbage and put a permanent lid on it.

Rabbi Marc S. Jagolinzer, in his editorial in *Clergy Corner,* says it best:

> True courage in life means letting go. Letting go takes
> courage because it means that you have to admit there are
> times in life when you are powerless and you cannot fix

everything. ... Letting go takes courage because it means that you no longer regret the past, but rather just try to live in the present and look to the future. ... It means that you learn that there are things that you just have to accept, and when you accept them, then you have the peace of mind and the courage to work on your own life.[37]

The second most-asked question we get is, "Can a marriage or relationship survive the betrayal of infidelity?" Conventional wisdom says if someone has cheated, call a killer lawyer, burn the marriage license, and look up your community property rights. But there's another school of thought that maintains that betrayal can be a first step in finally addressing the thorny issues hidden deep within a marriage.

Jane E. Brody, in her *New York Times* article, "When a Partner Cheats," notes, "the good news is depending upon what caused one partner to wander and how determined a couple is to remain together, infidelity need not result in divorce."[38]

Consistent with this finding, Esther Perel, therapist and author of *The State of Affairs: Rethinking Infidelity,* found that "Couples that choose to recover from and rebuild after infidelity often end up with a stronger, more loving, and mutually understanding relationship than they had previously."[39]

Good news, indeed.

And finally, Michele Weiner-Davis, author of *Healing from Infidelity: The Divorce Busting® Guide to Rebuilding Your Marriage After an Affair*, adds, "People who've been betrayed need to know that there's no shame in staying in the marriage. They're not doormats;

---

37 Jagolinzer, "Crisis is a Chance to Show Resilience."
38 Brody, "When a Partner Cheats."
39 Perel, *The State of Affairs: Rethinking Infidelity.*

they're warriors. The gift they provide to their families by working through the pain is enormous."[40]

In Chapter Seven, we talk about the pivot. Businesses often try out a new idea, fail fast, learn fast, and then fashion something new based on insights and learning from failure. The same holds true for relationships. In the same way, self-learning can be the positive result of marital betrayal. It is possible to pivot and divorce your old marriage and start anew with more honesty and openness. This pivot can result in a new and better model for success.

That's the upside. But what if you decide that no pivot is possible? Can you ever love again?

Jenny Sanford, former wife of Mark Sanford, the disgraced former governor of South Carolina, suffered a very painful and public betrayal. Jenny had a healthy and clear perspective about dating again. As she explains, "I would never trust anyone who did not treat me the way I deserved. Why would I ever let myself be treated badly? Why would I ever throw my pearls before swine?"[41]

Her elegant response divines a future of self-confidence, self-worth, and informed risk-taking. Again, we see the importance of trusting wisely because it can point you in the direction of a successful recovery.

Finally, we learned these survival techniques (listen to your gut, view stress as your friend, hold on to your power, and the find the courage to move on) are useful tools anytime, anywhere.

The next two stories illustrate how these tactics were used to successfully avoid a violation of organizational trust. Betrayal was kept at bay. Note that humor plays a role in the first, and a network of professional colleagues plays a role in the second.

---

40 Weiner-Davis, *Healing from Infidelity: The Divorce Busting® Guide to Rebuilding Your Marriage After an Affair.*

41 Sanford, *Staying True.*

LAUGHTER IS THE
BEST REVENGE

Debra was looking forward to being part of a board of distinguished directors. She respected the CEO, and he, in turn, was impressed by her position as chair of a billion-dollar company.

She had met all the directors before, with the exception of one. At her first meeting, she sat next to the very short man she had yet to meet. Despite her attempts to have a conversation with him, he completely ignored Debra, signaling disapproval with his eyes.

Not to be deterred, she placed her business card directly in front of him.

Astoundingly, he snapped it up and said, "You don't belong here. And neither does he," pointing to Daniel, the African-American director sitting across from them.

Debra didn't want to call attention to his rude behavior, so she packed this experience away. She thought it best to carefully plot her response, should this happen again.

The man's misogynistic and racist behavior continued in subsequent meetings, but Debra always made a point of joining his conversations. She never failed to respond politely to his curtness.

"Why do you even bother with him?" her board colleagues asked.

"Just trying to see what I can learn in spite of his issues with me," she answered.

But in truth, Debra was waiting for the right moment to deal with his nastiness.

It came at a board retreat, where Debra, Daniel, and the man in question were talking to the CEO about the possibility of adding new board members.

With a twinkle in her eye, she gestured to her nemesis and said to the CEO, "The only reason you have him on the board is, he's a midget. Add that to a woman and an African-American, and you've got all the diversity bases covered," she smiled.

The CEO roared with laughter.

You might question why we consider this example to exist at the beginning of the continuum of betrayal. Debra's reputation wasn't in danger, nor was the company facing an ethical threat. So why include it? Because Debra recognized the unfriendly board member as a potential menace who might well try to betray her. We label this story as a slight betrayal of organizational trust, due to the lack of professionalism and disrespect that the man showed Debra, despite the fact that they were fellow directors and she, therefore, deserved his respect.

Debra practiced strategic patience to neutralize the situation and resist the urge to protest his behavior right away. When the timing was right, she employed the effective tool of targeted humor to make a larger point.

Finally, here's a story of perfect timing that helped to derail a betrayal.

ALL THE WORLD'S A STAGE

Robert's love of the theater was boundless. Every aspect of production inspired him, which is why he was so thrilled to hear from his old colleague, Lindsay.

In the past, she headed the business end of a small, but nationally prominent theater, while he served as the artistic director. Their successful partnership had lasted almost a decade.

"Robert, there's a perfect opportunity for us to set up a theater program for a London-based university, and I can't imagine a better artistic director to have by my side than you."

Robert didn't have to think too long about this offer.

"It's ideal," he agreed.

So Robert forged ahead, organizing ideas, creating an action plan, and finding the best instructors. Lindsay suggested a stipend for each semester that Robert was in charge of the artistic side of the program.

"We'll nail down the details later," she reasoned. "Because there's so much for us to do to get this off the ground."

"Not a problem," Robert replied, as he rushed off to answer an email from one of his favorite acting instructors.

Several semesters later, Lindsay was in the middle of a debilitating divorce, and Robert was deeply troubled by her constant procrastination in regard to his contract.

As he entered her office for a long-overdue confrontation, Lindsay ambushed him with a stunning piece of news.

"I'm moving the program to a new venue," she said surprisingly. "It'll be better for the students."

"Not without a contract in advance," said Robert.

"Oh, absolutely, it's top of my list," Lindsay replied unconvincingly.

Out of the corner of his eye, Robert spotted a red flag waving.

Behind the scenes, Lindsay had negotiated a contract for herself. She told the new university she was completely in charge. They asked about Robert.

"Oh, with his reputation, he can fend for himself," Lindsay told them.

Robert wrote a long, detailed report to the university, citing his grievances and Lindsay's false promises. He copied Lindsay and the theater community on the report. A pro forma response came back from the university, with no action. After all, Robert was not under contract.

Luckily, the theatrical community rallied round Robert, hiring him for individual projects, which helped him find his footing.

Lindsay lost interest in the theater program when her hefty divorce *settlement arrived. And she lost her following when others saw her deceit.*

Today, Robert has created successful new programs for another prestigious university. But before he did any work, Robert signed a tight contract.

Robert understood that Lindsay had used their past relationship to take advantage of him. She had expected Robert to have a passive role in her drama, but he'd refused to play the part and become a victim.

Instead, he gathered his resources and reported the facts, and even though the university refused to take action, Robert's network of friends and colleagues saw the true picture. The fallout of total betrayal was averted. Robert was proactive and realistic, and as a result, he created a successful future.

We have learned from all our survivors that bad stuff happens to everyone. Hurt, setbacks, and diabolical events touch all of our lives. There is no escape. But inside all of us are the keys to unlock our courage and strength, and that's how we move on and build a better future. How you choose to use those keys is critical to your outcome. When you feel you've been run over by a train, let the dust settle, survey the landscape, and then ask yourself, "Do I have the courage to get back on my feet?"

Hint: The correct answer is "Yes! Of course I do!" One step at a time. One day, one week, one month. And you're on your way.

We wrote this book to give you the tools to deal with betrayal, to understand your experience, to prevent you from feeling responsible, to regain your self-confidence, and most importantly, to help you move forward with confidence and courage.

Because, overwhelmingly, our survivors' message is a simple one: "Choose courage."

About the Authors

ELAINE EISENMAN, PHD

A seasoned executive and longtime board director, Elaine Eisenman, PhD, currently serves as a director for DSW, Inc (NYSE), AtmosXR, and Miravan, both privately held companies. She is the managing director of Saeje Advisors, LLC, an advisory firm for high-growth ventures. She is also a senior advisor to IEC Partners, a global firm focused on helping non-US companies establish a US market and base. In addition, she works with the team at Entrepreneurship Policy Advisors to create and implement entrepreneurial ecosystems, focused on growing and scaling companies.

Dr. Eisenman has served on public company boards since 1996, when she joined the United States Tobacco board. At UST, she chaired the Compensation Committee and was on the Nominating and Governance Committee. She is currently a board member of DSW, Inc (NYSE), where she is a member of the Compensation and Nominating committees, and chairs the annual strategy review, also having served on the CEO selection committee. Until recently, she served on Board of Harvard Vanguard Health Associates (HVMA), a $1.5 billion non-profit health care organization, where she chaired the Compensation Committee and sat on the Executive Committee and the Strategic Initiatives Committee, as well as serving on HVMA's parent, Atrius Health, Compensation Committee and strategy committee. Elaine is also on the Advisory Board of Qwalify, a Canadian start-up. She has also served on the boards of several private companies, including Active International, an international barter company, and HRLogic, A Fidelity Capital start-up, and several family and early stage businesses. She is a founding member, chapter co-chair, and member of the Advisory Board of Women Corporate Directors Foundation, a high profile global organization for women public and private board members.

In 2011, she was selected by *Agenda* as a top 100 Diversity Board Member, and in 2012 she was named a "Director to Watch" by *Directors and Boards*.

Most recently, Dr. Eisenman served as dean of executive and enterprise education at Babson College, and professor of entrepreneurial leadership for twelve years. In her role, she developed and taught in a wide range of programs for entrepreneurs and corporate executives. She was also responsible for the management of award-winning Babson Executive Conference Center, a 250-bed hotel and conference facility, consistently rated by IACC as a top global facility.

Dr. Eisenman's career also includes experience as a business leader and general manager, HR executive, and organizational consultant. Her key areas of expertise include CEO succession and transition, and the alignment of strategy, selection, compensation, and performance during periods of growth, mergers, and transformation. She has consulted with a number of global companies including BMW, CSFB, Glaxo Smith Kline, Citibank, Marsh, ToysRUs, AT&T, Colgate Palmolive, Pepsi, American Express, Bank of America,

Barclays, Santander, as well as a number of rapidly growing mid and small cap companies.

Dr. Eisenman has held senior executive positions at both public companies such as American Express, Enhance Financial Services Co., and The Children's Place, and private companies such as PDI International, a global consulting firm, where she both built and was general manager of the Northeast region, and Management & Capital Partners, a retained executive recruitment, management consulting, and venture capital firm, where she was chairman.

Dr. Eisenman is coauthor of, *I Didn't See It Coming: The Only Book You'll Ever Need to Avoid Being Blindsided in Business*, published by John Wiley and Sons. Most recently, she was a commissioner of two WCD sponsored white papers entitled "Seeing Far and Wide" and "Moving towards a Visionary Board and The Visionary Board at Work: Developing a Culture of Leadership." She was also interviewed for a ninety-minute webinar co-sponsored by NACD and Pearl Meyer on the Board's role in supporting innovation, as well as for a webinar by FT on the same topic. She is frequently cited in articles featured in *Business Week*, *WSJ*, *Agenda*, *Directorship*, *Worth* and *Board Member*.

Dr. Eisenman earned a PhD in industrial/organizational psychology from New York University, an MS from Columbia University, and a BS from Boston University.

You can contact her at ElaineJEisenman.com.

SUSAN STAUTBERG

As governance advisor to Atlantic Street Capital, Susan launched the first private equity firm effort to recruit women for portfolio executive positions, company boards, and customer advisory boards.

Susan recently retired as chair and co-founder of the Women-CorporateDirectors (WCD) Foundation, the only global membership organization and community of women corporate directors. WCD has more than 2,500 members in eighty chapters around the world. She is the president and CEO of PartnerCom Corporation, and co-founded OnBoard Bootcamp (OBB), an insider's guide on how to be selected to a corporate, private company, or advisory board director position, and the Belizean Grove, a preeminent community and retreat for leading women who share knowledge and connections.

As a Westinghouse/Group W TV correspondent covering the White House and Capitol Hill, Susan was the first woman and one of the youngest to head a Washington TV bureau. Susan then became the first TV journalist to be chosen as a White House Fellow where she worked for both Vice President Nelson Rockefeller and Secretary of State Henry Kissinger. Her considerable consumer products experience includes positions as the director of communications for the US Consumer Product Safety Commission and for McNeil Consumer Products. Deciding to become an entrepreneur, Susan founded MasterMedia, Ltd., the only company to combine publishing with a speaker's bureau.

In her capacity as a corporate and nonprofit director, Susan has served on or created advisory boards, for numerous organizations. Susan has also served on Presidential Commissions, Boards, and Foundations. Susan is a board member of the Community Foundation for Palm Beach and Martin Counties. Susan's active involvement in The Preservation Society of Newport County is longstanding; currently she chairs The Elms Committee and was a member of the Capital Campaign Council. She is also a member of the C200, International Women's Forum, and the Council on Foreign Relations.

Susan holds a BA from Wheaton College, and an MA in public

and international affairs from George Washington University, and she completed an Executive Education Program at Harvard Business School. She addresses groups around the world, including leading business schools and national and international conferences. Her writing consists of seven books, including *Betrayed: A Survivors Guide to Lying, Cheating & Double Dealing*; *Women on Board: Insider Secrets to Getting on a Board and Succeeding as a Director*; and *Selected Quotations that Inspire Us to Think Bigger, Live Better and Laugh Harder*.

She has written or been featured in numerous articles including *International Herald Tribune*, *Businessweek*, *The New York Times*, *The Wall Street Journal*, *Directors and Boards*, *The Financial Times*, and others. Her on-air interview experience includes CNBC, *Oprah*, *The Today Show*, *CBS Evening News*, CNN, and many others.

Susan has received numerous awards and honors including an Honorary Doctorate of Law from Wheaton College, and WCD's Visionary Award for Strategic Leadership.

Harvard Business School is writing a case study on how Susan and co-founders created WCD and sold it to KPMG which has turned it into a non-profit.

You can contact her at SusanSStautberg.com.

Contact Us

Susan Stautberg and Elaine Eisenman are available for speeches and seminars. For further information on availability and fee arrangements, visit them at:

SusanSStautberg.com
ElaineJEisenman.com

Book Club Questions

1. Have you read anything about this topic before? How much did you know about this book's topic?

2. How does this book relate to your life experiences? Do the survivors' stories seem authentic? Can you relate to their predicaments? How would you react if you were in one of these situations? Has anything like this happened to you? How did you deal with it?

3. What feelings did the book evoke? Did the book make you feel uncomfortable or relieved? What struck you as significant? Amusing? Sad? Illuminating? Disturbing? What was memorable? What resonated with you?

4. Which story was most relatable? Why did you connect with it? Which story troubled you the most, and why do you think this was true?

5. How did the book affect you? Do you feel "changed" in any way? Did it challenge your assumptions? Expand your knowledge? Change your perspective or opinion? After reading it, did it help you better understand yourself or another person? Did this give you a new awareness about your own life?

6. What songs does this book make you think of? Create a playlist with your fellow members.

7. If you could ask the authors one question, what would it be? If you could ask the survivors one question, who would it be and what question?

8. Do you think any of the stories could be made into a full-length book or movie? Which ones and why?

9. Are the authors solutions/recommendations sensible/concrete and implementable? Any other ideas/option you might suggest?

10. Were there any stories where you disagreed with the choices the survivors made? Which ones? And what would have done differently?

Bibliography

Ackerman, Bonnie G. "You Had Me at 'I'm Sorry': The Impact of Physicians' Apologies of Medical Malpractice Litigation." *The National Law Review,* November 6, 2018. https://www.natlawreview.com/article/you-had-me-i-m-sorry-impact-physicians-apologies-medical-malpractice-litigation

Ashkenas, Ron, and Holly Newman. "Learn to Trust Your Gut." *Harvard Business Review,* January 31, 2012. https://hbr.org/2012/01/learn-to-trust-your-gut.html.

Babiak, Paul, and Robert Hare. *Snakes in Suits: When Psychopaths Go to Work.* HarperCollins, 2006.

Beam, Cris. "I Did a Terrible Thing. How Can I Apologize?" *New York Times.* June 30, 2018.

Bénabou, Roland, and Jean Tirole. "Identity, Morals, and Taboos: Beliefs as Assets." *The Quarterly Journal of Economics* 126, no. 2 (May 2011): 805-855. https://doi.org/10.1093/qje/qjr002.

"Betrayal: The Emotional Malady of Family Businesses – Parts One and Two." *Hubler For Business Families.* July 17, 2017. www.hublerfamilybusiness.com/blog.

"Betrayal Trauma." *Encyclopedia of Psychological Trauma*, 1ˢᵗ edition. 2008.

Brody, Jane E. "When a Partner Cheats." *New York Times*. January 22, 2018. https://www.nytimes.com/2018/01/22/well/marriage-cheating-infidelity. html.

Brown, Theresa. "How to Quantify a Nurse's Gut Feelings." *New York Times*, August 9, 2018. https://www.nytimes.com/2018/08/09/opinion/sunday/ nurses-gut-feelings-rothman.html.

Bruehl, Sam, and Rob Lachenauer. "How Family Business Owners Should Bring the Next Generation into the Company." *Harvard Business Review*. July 24, 2018. https://hbr.org/2018/07/how-family-business-owners-should-bring-the-next-generation-into-the-company.

Caldwell, Cam, and Ranjan Karri. "Organizational Governance and Ethical Systems: A Covenantal Approach to Building Trust." *Journal of Business Ethics* 58, no. 1–3 (April–May 2005): 249-259. https://doi.org/ 10.1007/ s10551-005-1419-2.

Caldwell, Cam, and Rolf D. Dixon. "Love, Forgiveness, and Trust: Critical Values of the Modern Leader." *Journal of Business Ethics* 93, no. 1 (April 2010): 91-101. https://doi.org/10.1007/s10551-009-0184-z.

Carlsmith, Kevin M., et al. "The Paradoxical Consequences of Revenge." *Journal of Personality and Social Psychology* 95, no. 6 (December 2008): 1316–24. https://doi.org/10.1037/a0012165.

Carmichael, Kay. "The Rhetoric of Trust and the Silence of Betrayal." *Hume Papers on Public Policy* 7, no. 3 (September 1999): 53.

Cather, Willa. *The Song of the Lark*. Houghton Mifflin Company, 1915.

Chabris, Christopher, and Daniel Simons. *The Invisible Gorilla*. New York City: Harmony Publishers, 2011.

Clark, Alicia H. *Hack Your Anxiety*. Sourcebooks, 2018.

Cobb, Anthony T., et al. "The Role Justice Plays in Organizational Change." *Public Administration Quarterly* 19, no. 2 (1995): 135-151.

Cohen, Adam. "Research on the Science of Forgiveness: An Annotated Bibliography: Summaries of Research on Forgiveness, Peace, and Well-being." *Greater Good Magazine*. October 1, 2004, www.greatergood.berkeley.edu/article/item/the_science_of_forgiveness_an_annotated_bibliography.

Coleman, Joshua. "Surviving Betrayal." *Greater Good Magazine*. September 1, 2008. www.greatergood.berkeley.edu/article/item/surviving_betrayal.

Costigan, Robert D., et al. "A Multi-Dimensional Study of Trust in Organizations." *Journal of Managerial Issues* 10, no. 3 (1998): 303-317.

Cox, Caroline. "Ever Wanted to Get Revenge? Try This Instead." *New York Times*. July 19, 2018. www.nytimes.com/2018/07/19/smarter-living/how-to-turn-toxic-emotions-into-positiveactions.html.

Degadt, Jan. "Business Family and Family Business: Complementary and Conflicting Values." *Journal of Enterprising Culture* 11, no. 4 (2003): 379–397. https://doi.org/10.1142/S0218495803000135

Dickinson, Kirra. "How Mindfulness Can Help Us Forgive Betrayal." *Greater Good Magazine*. April 20, 2016. www.greatergood.berkeley.edu/article/item/how_mindfulness_helps_us_forgive_betrayal.

Dirks, Kurt T., and Donald L. Ferrin. "The Role of Trust in Organizational Settings." *Organization Science* 12, no. 4 (July—August 2001): 450-467.

Dutton, Kevin. *The Wisdom of Psychopaths: What Saints, Spies, and Serial Killers Can Teach Us About Success*. Scientific American / Farrar, Straus and Giroux, 2012.

Elangovan, A.R., and Debra L. Shapiro. "Betrayal of Trust in Organizations." *The Academy of Management Review* 23, no. 3 (July 1998): 547-566.

"Family Business Succession and Planning." *Family Business Institute White Paper*, January 2018.

Fisher, Cynthia D., and Neal M. Ashkanasy. "The Emerging Role of Emotions in Work Life: An Introduction." *Emotions in Organization* special issue of *Journal of Organizational Behavior* 21, no. 2 (March 2000): 123-129.

Fitness, Julie. "Anger in the Workplace: An Emotion Script Approach to Anger Episodes Between Workers and Their Superiors, Co-Workers and Subordinates." *Emotions in Organization,* special issue of *Journal of Organizational Behavior* 21, no. 2 (March 2000): 147-162.

—— "Betrayal, Rejection, Revenge, and Forgiveness: An Interpersonal Script Approach." *Interpersonal Rejection*, Leary, M. (Ed.) 2001. 73-103.

Fletcher, Denise, editor. *Understanding the Small Family Business*. Routledge, 2002. *EBSCO Online Database Business Source Complete*. Accessed 26 Apr. 2007.

Freyd, Jennifer J., and Pamela J. Birrell. *Blind to Betrayal*. John Wiley & Sons, 2013.

Funk, Liz. "The Hidden Power in Trusting Your Gut Instincts." *Fast Company.* April 7, 2016. www.fastcompany.com/3058609/the-hidden-power-in-trusting-your-gut-instincts.

Galford, Robert M., and Anne Seibold Drapeau. "The Enemies of Trust." *Harvard Business Review*, Feb.2003.

Haley, Jay. *Uncommon Therapy: The Psychiatric Techniques of Milton H. Erickson, M.D.* 2nd ed., W. W. Norton & Company, 1993.

Halonen, Susanna M. "3 Reasons Why You Have to Trust Your Gut: When and How to Use Your Intuition." *Psychology Today*. May 20 2015. www. psychologytoday.com/us/blog/the-path-passionate-happiness/201505/3-reasons-why-you-have-trust-your-gut.

Haney, John Mark, and Leslie Hardie. "Psychotherapeutic Considerations for Working With Betrayed Spouses: A Four-Task Recovery Model." *Australian and New Zealand Journal of Family Therapy* 35, no. 4 (December 2014): 401-413,doi.org/10.1002/anzf.1073.

Hannah, Sophie. *How to Hold a Grudge*. Simon & Schuster, 2018.

Hannon, Peggy A., et al. "In the Wake of Betrayal: Amends, Forgiveness, and the Resolution of Betrayal." *Personal Relationships: Journal of the International Association for Relationship Research* 17, no. 2 (June 2010): 253–278.

Hanover, Donna. *My Boyfriend's Back: True Stories of Rediscovering Love with Long-Lost Sweethearts*. Listen & Live Audio, Inc., 2005.

Harra, Carmen. "13 Steps to Recover From Betrayal." *HuffPost*. August 8, 2014. https://www.huffpost.com/entry/14-steps-to-recover-from_b_5660057.

Hayes, Steven, and Spencer Smith. *Get Out of Your Mind and Into Your Life: The New Acceptance and Commitment Therapy*. New Harbinger Publications, 2005.

Heffernan, Margaret. *Willful Blindness*. Walker & Co. Publishers, 2011.

Heitler, Susan, and Laurie Moore. "22 Ways Couples Can Survive Cheating (And Finally Heal From the Betrayal)." *Your Tango Blog*. February 15, 2018. https://www.yourtango.com/experts/ yourtango-experts/22-ways-couples-can-overcome-infidelity-expert.

Hoy, Wayne K., and Megan Tschannen-Moran. "A Multidisciplinary Analysis of the Nature, Meaning, and Measurement of Trust." *Review of Educational Research* 70, no. 4 (2000): 547-593.

Jagolinzer, Rabbi Marc S. "Crisis is a Chance to Show Resilience" *Clergy Corner. The Newport Daily News.* 10, 2014. https://www.newportri.com/5e53a1d7-c98a-527e-9c51-14bb16a25537.html.

Jones, David A. "Getting Even with One's Supervisor and One's Organization: Relationships Among Types of Injustice, Desires for Revenge, and Counterproductive Work Behaviors." *Journal of Organizational Behavior* 30, no. 4 (May 2009): 525-542.

Karl, Katherine A. *The Academy of Management Executive (1993-2005)* 18, no. 1 (2004): 138-140. JSTOR, www.jstor.org/stable/4166053.

Kaufman, Peter, and Janine, Schipper. *Teaching with Compassion: An Educator's Oath to Teach from the Heart.* Rowman & Littlefield, 2018.

Ketteler, Judi. "How to Get Your Intuition Back (When It's Hijacked by Life)." *New York Times.* July 17, 2018. www.nytimes.com/2018/07/17/well/intuition-gut-instinct-psychology-midlifecrisis.html.

Khazan, Olga. "The Forgiveness Boost." *The Atlantic.* January 28, 2015. https://www.theatlantic.com/health/archive/2015/01/the-forgiveness-boost/384796/.

Kidder, Deborah L. "Is It 'Who I Am', 'What I Can Get Away with', or 'What You've Done to Me'? A Multi Theory Examination of Employee Misconduct." *Journal of Business Ethics* 57, no. 4 (April 2005): 389-398.

King, Martin Luther, 1929-1968 and Clayborne Carson. *Stride Toward Freedom: The Montgomery Story.* Beacon Press, 2010.

Krebs, Dennis L. "Morality: An Evolutionary Account." *Perspectives on Psychological Science* 3, no. 3 (May 2008): 149-172.

Levinson, Harry. "Conflicts That Plague Family Businesses." *Harvard Business Review.* March 1971. www.hbr.org/1971/03/conflicts-that-plague-family-businesses%201/19. Accessed July 31, 2018.

Lewicki, Roy J., et al. "Trust and Distrust: New Relationships and Realities." *The Academy of Management Review* 23, no. 3 (July 1998): 438-458.

McGonigal, Kelly. "How To Make Stress Your Friend." TED|Global, 2013. https:// www.ted.com/talks/ kelly_mcgonigal_how_to_make_stress_your_friend?

McLain, David L., and Katrina Hackman. "Trust, Risk, and Decision-Making in Organizational Change." *Public Administration Quarterly* 23, no. 2 (1999): 152-176.

Means, Benjamin. "Non-Market Values in Family Business." *William and Mary Law Review* 54, no. 4 (2013): 1185-1250.

Miller, Marissa. "Turning a Breakup into a Positive Experience." *New York Times.* June 19, 2018. https://www.nytimes.com/2018/06/19/smarter-living/ turning-a-breakup-into-a-positive-experience.html.

Moberg, Dennis J. "On Employee Vice." *Business Ethics Quarterly* 7, no. 4 (October 1997): 41-60.

Perel, Esther. *The State of Affairs: Rethinking Infidelity.* HarperCollins, 2017.

Palanski, Michael E. "Forgiveness and Reconciliation in the Workplace: A Multi-Level Perspective and Research Agenda." *Journal of Business Ethics* 109, no. 3 (September 2012): 275-287.

Pascal, Blaise. *Thoughts*, translated by W. F. Trotter. Vol. XLVIII, Part 1. *The Harvard Classics.* New York: P.F. Collier & Son, 1909–14; Bartleby.com, 2001, www.bartleby.com/48/1.

Patton, Bailey. "The Role of Forgiveness in Mediating Feelings of Betrayal within Older Adult Romantic Relationships." *GRASP: Graduate Research and Scholarly Projects* [Wichita State University] 9, 2013.

Poniewozik, James, Hale, Mike, Lyons, Margaret. "Best TV Episodes of 2018." *The New York Times*. December 24, 2018. https://www.nytimes.com/2018/12/24/arts/television/best-tv-episodes-of-2018.html

Price, Michael. "Revenge and the People Who Seek It: New Research Offers Insight into the Dish Best Served Cold." *Monitor on Psychology, the Magazine of the American Psychological Association* 40, no. 6 (2009): 34.

Pulda, Molly. "Unknown Knowns: State Secrets and Family Secrets." *Biography* 35, no. 3 (2012): 472-491.

Rachman, S. "Betrayal: A Psychological Analysis." *Behaviour Research and Therapy* 48, no. 4 (April 2010): 304–311.

Rachman, S., et al. "Mental Contamination: The Perpetrator Effect." *Journal of Behavior Therapy and Experimental Psychiatry* 43, no. 1 (March 2012): 587-593. doi.org/10.1016/j.jbtep.2011.08.002.

Reina, Dennis, and Michelle L. Reina. *Trust & Betrayal in the Workplace: Building Effective Relationships in Your Organization*. 3rd ed., Berrett-Koehler Publishers, 2015.

Roscigno, Vincent J., et al. "Workplace Incivilities: The Role of Interest Conflicts, Social Closure and Organizational Chaos." *Work, Employment & Society* 23, no. 4 (December 2009): 747-773.

Rose, Carol M. "Trust in the Mirror of Betrayal." *Yale Law School Faculty Scholarship Series*, 1 Jan. 1995.

Sandberg, Sheryl, and Adam Grant. *Facing Adversity, Building Resilience, and Finding Joy*. Knopf, 2017.

Sanford, Jenny. *Staying True*. Ballantine Books, 2010.

Sauerheber, Jill Duba, and J. Graham Disque. "A Trauma-Based Physiological Approach: Helping Betrayed Partners Heal from Marital Infidelity." *The Journal of Individual Psychology* 72, no. 3 (2016).

Seabright, Mark A., and Marshall Schminke. "Immoral Imagination and Revenge in Organizations: At Our Best: Moral Lives in a Moral Community." *Journal of Business Ethics* 38, no. 1-2 (June 2002): 19-31.

Silber, Debi. "Getting Past the Pain Of Betrayal Requires this Subtle But Dramatic Shift." *Your Tango Blog.* September 21, 2018. www.yourtango. com/experts/debi-silber/what-does-betrayal-mean-how-to-recover-from-trauma-being-betrayed-in-love-relationships.

Stalk, George, and Henry Foley. "Avoid the Traps That Can Destroy Family Businesses." *Harvard Business Review,* January-Febuary. 2012.

Stein, Howard F. "Organizational Euphemism and the Cultural Mystification of Evil." *Administrative Theory & Praxis* 20, no. 3, (September 1998): 346-357.

Stosny, Steven. "Anger in the Age of Entitlement. Learning to Trust Wisely." *Psychology Today.* January 3, 2014. www.psychologytoday.com/us/blog/anger-in-the-age-entitlement/201401/trust-and-Betrayal.

"Anger in the Age of Entitlement. Living and Loving Again. Forgiveness After Betrayal." *Psychology Today.* December 4, 2013. www.psychologytoday. com/us/blog/anger-in-the-age-entitlement/201312.

Stout, Martha. *The Sociopath Next Door.* Harmony, 2006.

Streep, Peg. "The Psychology of Revenge (and Vengeful People)." *Psychology Today.* July 19, 2017. www.psychologytoday.com/us/blog/tech-support/201707/the-psychology-revenge-and-vengeful-people.

Suazo, Mark M. "The Impact of Affect and Social Exchange on Outcomes of Psychological Contract Breach." *Journal of Managerial Issues* 23, no. 2 (2011): 190-205.

Syms, Marcy. *Mind Your Own Business and Keep It in the Family.* Master Media Pub Corp, 1992.

Tetteh, Vanessa A. "Family Business Strategy." *Research Starters: Business (Online Edition)*, 2013.

Thompson, Merideth J., et al. "We All Seek Revenge: The Role of Honesty-Humility in Reactions to Incivility." *Journal of Behavioral and Applied Management* 17, no. 1 (December 2016).

Trafford, Abigail. *Crazy Time.* 3rd ed., Morrow Publishers, 2014.

Warschaw, Tessa Albert, and Dee Barlow. *Resiliency: How to Bounce Back Faster, Stronger, Smarter.* Master Media Pub Corp, 1995.

Weiner-Davis, Michele. *Source Healing from Infidelity: The Divorce Busting® Guide to Rebuilding Your Marriage After an Affair.* Michele Weiner-Davis Training Corporation, 2017.

Wells, Carole V., and David Kipnis. "Trust, Dependency, and Control in the Contemporary Organization." *Journal of Business and Psychology* 15, no. 4 (March 2001): 593-603.

Westberg, Granger E. *Good Grief.* Fortress Press, 2011. Master Media Pub Corp.

Widmann, Nancy, Elaine Eisenman, and Amy Kopelan. *I Didn't See it Coming: The Only Book You'll Ever Need to Avoid Being Blindsided in Business.* John Wiley and Sons, 2007.